# St. George
# and the Dandelion

# St. George
# and the Dandelion

40 Years of Practice as a Jungian Analyst

by Joseph B. Wheelwright

Preface by Erik H. Erikson
Foreword by Gregory Bateson
Edited by Audrey Hilliard Blodgett

C. G. Jung Institute of San Francisco, Inc.

58·744

Copyright © 1982 The C. G. Jung Institute of San Francisco, Inc.

Published by the C. G. Jung Institute of San Francisco, Inc., 2040 Gough Street, San Francisco, California 94109

Abbreviation of Principal Reference

CW = *The Collected Works of C. G. Jung*. Edited by Gerhard Adler, Michael Fordham, and Herbert Read; William McGuire, Executive Editor; translated by R. F. C. Hull; New York and Princeton (Bollingen Series XX) and London, 1953–1978. 20 vols. References are to paragraph numbers.

Library of Congress Cataloging in Publication Data
Wheelwright, Joseph B., 1906–
  St. George and the dandelion.
  Includes bibliographical references and index.
  1. Wheelwright, Joseph B., 1906–
  2. Psychoanalysts—United States—Biography.
  3. Jung, C. G. (Carl Gustav), 1875–1961. 4. Psycho-
analysis. I. Blodgett, Audrey Hilliard. II. Title.
RC339.52.W48A37    150.19'54'0924    81-13672
ISBN 0-932630-04-9    AACR2

Printed in the United States of America

Jacket photograph: Richard Lee Schoenbrun
Jacket and page design: Dorothy Sibley
Typography: Bembo and Galliard by Abracadabra
Printing: Maple Vail

*To Jane, Lynda, and John*

# Contents

# Preface

Neither my friend Joseph Wheelwright, nor his book, needs a "preface." He is an acknowledged leader in the Jungian establishment and a beloved teacher and practitioner in psychiatry. I am writing only as a spokesman for his friends and students, who are convinced that one has to have seen Jo Wheelwright to believe him and that one has to have heard him to read him. For he writes as he speaks; and it is his editor's merit that she preserves his way of crowning the discussion of exalted concepts and of intimate clinical experience with pungent personal remarks.

As to his appearance, you cannot avoid looking up to the man if you want to come face to face with him. For he is very tall and lean; and in conversation, he persuasively lowers himself toward you. His accent has strong Bostonian and British overtones that, however, pass the test of serving with equal naturalness both thoughtful discourse and exquisite vulgarity. And his aristocratic height does not interfere with his suddenly leaning into any available piano and hammering away in the best worst barroom style.

In fact, to overdo this aspect of the man a little, one of my earlier memories of him is a scene at a party where he joined a rather short Freudian, our late friend Donald "Mac" Macfarlane, at a piano for an especially lowbrow duet. Jo, too, remembers this event because in the stunned silence that followed their performance he heard me murmur, "A Freudian and a Jungian meeting on the lowest common denominator." He appreciated my ecumenical spirit. And, unnecessary to say, we Freudians have over the years met with this Jungian on high common denominators indeed. But I am glad to report this event because in this instance I for once recognize myself in a quotation ascribed to me by Jo.

Of our joint professional activities, two stand out. During the Second World War we participated in the Mt. Zion Veterans' Rehabilitation Clinic. There, we (and others representing an assortment of psychiatric denominations) found that in dealing with the problems of returned combat soldiers, we could quietly amalgamate our various views and personalities in a communal common sense. And, to return to the present, when the Freud-Jung correspondence appeared, Jo and I enjoyed offering a public dialogue on this eventually tragic subject, conveying to our colleagues some of the subsequent history that we, in our younger years, had been privileged to witness.

This said, I can leave to the reader the experience of finding out that Jo Wheelwright—whatever his Jungian "type"—always conveys the experiential power of living and thinking and thus invites a direct and sturdy understanding of clinical and theoretical issues vital to our work and our time.

Erik H. Erikson

# Foreword

Inever know how to evaluate what Jo says about Jungian theory. The trouble is that I always feel better when he's coming
even before he comes into the room and before he has any
chance to apply theory. How do you trust a theory of psycho-
therapy when the practitioner makes you feel better without practicing?

To tell the truth I always wonder about Jung's contribution to
the whole business. All the Jungians that I know are kind, sensitive, imaginative, and, in a word, loving people. Perhaps it is so
that Carl Jung's achievement was in changing them to be that way
or perhaps his genius was in selection. Anyhow I always feel that I
can relax when I am with Jungians, and if you want to know why
this is so, you can just read this book and savor the syntax (or lack

of it) of any half dozen consecutive sentences. I often don't know what Jo is talking about, but I do know from the way he writes and the way he talks that he is a great and simple man.

I recall midnight in the Stanford Hospital in 1960. The surgeons had been at work on my diaphragm, and I was newly out of the intensive treatment ward with lots of cramps in my belly and no sureness that I'd live or wanted to live. I heard a commotion in the corridor, someone joshing the nurses in a most unmedical manner, and not just one wisecrack but a barrage of them, proceeding down the corridor in the direction of my ward. It was, of course, Jo, four hours after visiting time. Within a few minutes of his arrival the cramps disappeared, and after he had been with me 20 minutes, I was in the first sweet sleep since the operation. Well, that's Jungian theory at work, and I've no idea why it works unless perhaps it be a solvent for all of that nonsense of daily life that inhibits the communication of love.

I recall an odd little conference of psychiatrists who met one night in Berkeley to discuss "Aging." It was mostly a psychoanalytic group with a Freudian majority, and I do not now remember how I came to be there. The Freudians were moping about how when they grew old they would lose sexual potency, and then there would be no point in life. Jo and I were in a minority, agreeing with Rabbi Ben Ezra that the best is yet to be. Anyhow, that was nearly 30 years ago, and Jo and I are still happily kicking the daisies from on top.

He's more eager than I for new sensory experiences. Jane and he are going to Egypt next month, or is it Alaska? And a few months ago they were in Kenya, or was it the Valley of the Kings? Or scrambling through the paleolithic caves in the Pyrenees. He seems to have an uneconomical habit, an uneconomical greed—or it is a generous openness—for more and more raw data. I take it in, boil it down, and make it into theories, and after that I'm interested only in experiences that will contradict my theories. But Jo doesn't make theory; he keeps on being interested in more and more richness of detail.

"On Ilkley Moor bar t'at." I never know whether Jo is hiding behind the perpetual flow of humor, or is the humor really some sort of surfacing of Jungian theory, the top of the iceberg perhaps? It is certainly often an interruption, but if, when it has interrupted me, I take a look at what I would have said if I had not been interrupted, I usually find that it would have been a little heavy, a little dull, a little intellectual. The trouble with Jo—and I suspect this is also true in the therapy room—is that he is quicker than his patients' neuroses. They were just going to behave symptomatically when they find the consulting room has suddenly been invaded by a barroom piano and a ribald Yorkshire ditty. I guess it is disrupting for the patient to have the context of his next nonsense shifted before he gets there, but I suspect it may be therapeutic.

We don't know a thing about humor. A little perhaps about wit and *Schadenfreude*. Freud himself has told us a good deal about the jokes whose locus is on the edge of the incisors. We know nothing about the joking whose locus is in the belly or perhaps in dancing feet. A meticulous and scholarly study of Jo's book will convince the reader that there is something more than hostility in real humor, and that something more is balm for the human soul.

Gregory Bateson
Esalen
September 24, 1979

# St. George
# and the Dandelion

# *Imprimis*

Since my arrival on the Jungian scene in 1932, there has been a great burgeoning of ideas, proliferation of analysts and widening of their geographical distribution. Much of the impetus for this development continues to derive from Jung. It was gratifying that he was able to see, at the first Congress of the International Association for Analytical Psychology in 1958, how far and how deep his personality and his never-ending germination had carried. The papers given at the third Congress in 1965 reveal a trend that I think Jung would have approved of. He always inveighed against the dangers of over-organization and over-identification with an orthodoxy.

Not identifying with an orthodoxy is the more difficult warning to heed, particularly for those of us who were analyzed by

Jung, or who worked closely with him through the years. But time and geography are leading the younger analysts in new directions. Concepts tend to be modified by collaboration with related disciplines and by the widely varying contexts in which we live. *Au fond,* we are no less Jungian because of response to outer and relevant circumstances. In fact, it seems to me that stultification can be avoided only by healthy dissidence and dissonance. I think that the range of ideas in the following chapters honors this fact, without betraying the basic attitudes and values that attracted us to Jung in the first place.

I should like to acknowledge a number of people who have been important in the making of this book. First, were it not for Jack Buehler, who taped my seminars at Langley Porter Neuropsychiatric Institute, much of what follows would have been lost. Audrey Blodgett and I worked from transcriptions of those tapes in developing the manuscript. For their critical reading of the manuscript and many helpful suggestions, I extend thanks to my friends and colleagues, Katherine Bradway, Thomas Kirsch, Donald Sandner, Louis Stewart, and James Yandell; also to Joan Alpert, Librarian of the C. G. Jung Institute of San Francisco, to my daughter and colleague, Lynda Schmidt, and to my wife and colleague, Jane. To Gareth Hill and Barbara McClintock, I extend my special appreciation and thanks for their final editing, footnoting, and preparation of the manuscript for publication, and my thanks to Holly Reppert for her typing, and to Mary Hood for compiling the index. Finally, my gratitude to all members of the Institute for their support of this project.

*Bon Appetit!*

Joseph B. Wheelwright
Kentfield, California
January, 1981

# Exordium:[1]
# The Dandelion

## Origins

I came from a very conservative family, but I was heavily influenced by my wife's uncle, Lincoln Steffens. Steffie was a muckraking journalist, a pretty radical fellow. Through him we met many of the great radical intellectuals of the twenties—people like Clarence Darrow and Theodore Dreiser and Upton Sinclair.

I went to Harvard and might have gone to graduate school (though French literature and music were the only subjects I was good in), but I was expelled. Actually, I was kicked out twice, once after my freshman year and then for good after my junior year.

---

1. The beginning of anything, especially the introductory part of a discourse, treatise, etc.

My first big decision was whether to take a job with Fred Waring's Pennsylvanians at $100 a week or to teach school at $100 a month. Being a good Bostonian I took the more painful and less-well-paying job and became a schoolteacher.

Later I became a muckraking journalist myself. For a while I was in Shanghai working for an English-language paper called the *North China Daily News*. My reporting caused enough of a stir to get me thrown out of Shanghai. I had written articles exposing the terrible conditions in the spinning mills, and the Shanghai Municipal Council gave me three days to leave town.

Eighteen months later I went to Russia. It was a tremendously exciting place at the time (1932). There was that great sense of intoxication that emerges when people are working together at something really new and hopeful, something they care passionately about. (Of course later it became one more hierarchical, authoritarian society like ours. After the Moscow trials, when Stalin simply killed off his opponents, I became pretty disillusioned with Russia.)

Meanwhile my wife, Jane, had an aunt who developed schizophrenia. This turned out to be a real boon for us because the aunt's husband was taking her around to see the "crowned heads," as we called them (Freud, Adler, and Jung), and they landed in Zürich. Since Manchuria was being invaded, Jane had returned to California from China with our infant daughter. Six months later, she got to Zürich, acting as nurse for the schizophrenic aunt. I rejoined her there from Moscow.

Actually I was trying to get to Vienna to see the other master, but Jung wanted to interview us about the aunt, so we went to see him. And within the next thirteen or fourteen minutes—or perhaps seconds—all the little bells began to ring in my head, and suddenly I'd changed my plans quite radically. I thought, "I'm not going to go to Vienna at all," because the kind of person this man was and the kind of values he had seemed so good to me.

At that time I still didn't know quite what I wanted to do with my life. I'd been fortunate enough to have my father go bankrupt and to have been fired from Harvard, and these were two very forward-looking things that did a lot for me, but they didn't do it all. Then, I had had the great good fortune to find Jane. That was an enormous piece of luck, but there was one little problem. A large unconscious part of me was still looking around for a nice mummy who'd pat my head and blow my nose in adversity, but Jane wasn't keen on the mummy-business; that was, of course, one of the conscious reasons I had picked her, but my unconscious wasn't so convinced.

The real turning point came after I'd had a few analytic sessions with Jung, which had activated things in my psyche. Jane and I were down in Firenze staying in a third-class hotel, the Albergo something-or-other, where we had a room up under the roof somewhere. It was in early spring, and we'd been pounding around on those cold stone pavements in the Pitti Palace and the Uffizi, looking at the billowing Titians and one thing and another. When we got back to the hotel I didn't feel very well, so Jane fished a thermometer out of her reticule. Then we saw why I didn't feel very well: my temperature was 106! I wasn't a doctor at the time (I can hardly be described as one now), but I had read in books that if your temperature went over 106, you wrote to your family and ordered a box, so I realized that I wasn't well. Jane rushed out in a terrible state and got a doctor who came in and fiddled around, gave me some chalk or something, talked in French (my French wasn't too racy at the time, but his was worse), and left. I tried to prepare myself for death as best I could, and I fell into a kind of fitful delirium, or whatever you call it, and had a fantasy that I'd had many times before.

The fantasy went like this: Jane and I were driving along in a car, and suddenly a tire blew, or something happened, and the car went off the road and down a cliff end over end. Somehow or other Jane was unhurt, and she dragged me—all mashed up, legs wrapped about my neck, squirting blood in every direction—out of this mess and nursed me back to life. Well, in Firenze with a temperature of 106, I did better. I went over a cliff as usual, only this time *I* was the one who pulled *her* out of the wreck, and *I* was the one who nursed *her* back to life. Now that may not sound like anything to sway the Empire State Building, but for me it was the turning point. From that point on there was never any question in my mind about what the Good Lord had in mind for me to do, and what I wanted to do, and what I could do.

By this time I had had maybe a dozen sessions with Jung, and I realized that what he did was what I would like to do. As I have said, I had worked with little people as a schoolteacher, and then I had become terribly involved in social reform. My concern had been with people right along, but it was with people on paper and people *en masse*. Now I wanted to get back to people in the flesh, and this time I didn't want it to be children; I wanted it to be grown-ups. I wasn't altogether conscious, but that was the thread running underneath.

So I went back to Zürich, touched my forelock and said, "Dr. Jung, sir, I know I'm kind of neurotic, but do you think if we chipped away at it, that someday I might, uh, do what you do?" He said that was what everyone he analyzed wanted; it was just transference. And I said, "Goddam it, it's not just transference! What I really care about is people, all kinds of people: old, young, tall, short, thin, fat."

Well, he both encouraged me and discouraged me. He said I was so undisciplined that if I didn't go to medical school, he couldn't predict any future at all. He certainly wasn't terribly encouraging, and I really don't think he thought I would stay the course at medical school, and I wasn't too damn sure I would either. I had to do a year of pre-med, and at that time in England, where I planned to take my training, the medical course was five years, so it was to be a six-year stint altogether. But on a sort of blind faith I just went. I really struggled very hard at it and made it through.

In the interim I kept going back to Zürich every year for a month or so. Some years I went a couple of times, so I could keep badgering Jung and reminding him that I was going to qualify somewhere around 1938, and would he please just keep a space for me. He never made me any promises, and I very nearly didn't make it at the end, but thank the Lord I finally did.

When at last I returned to Zürich with my medical degree, I got an appointment with Jung, and he said, "I can't take you; I'm too busy."

I said, "Look, I have been badgering you for six years."

"Yes, I know. I know you have."

"It is enormously important to me."

"Well, you know, people say that, but we all have to do what we can do. I might see you one more time; you could go and see my secretary about it if you like."

His secretary was a young woman named Marie-Jeanne Schmid, a very nice person who was always very sweet to me and who really helped me a lot. She gave me an appointment, and then she said, "I'll just make you a series of appointments right along." Jung seemed a little puzzled as to why I kept coming back, but he had forgotten and really got into the work with me.

## Galaxy

I can't conceive of getting up in the morning without quite a few people around. I need to have Freud around; I need to have Jung around; I need to have Frieda Fromm-Reichmann, whom I knew and loved, around; I need to have Erik Erikson, who's a very dear friend, around; and then, I need *me* around. And if this galaxy of people isn't there, I'm not going to do very well that day. That is, I'm not much of a cultist; I rather distrust that kind of thing. I have a fairly catholic overlook, I think. I'm a Jungian analyst, because I find more that speaks to me in Jung's notions—primarily in his attitudes and his values—but if I've had a hobbyhorse I've been riding through these years, I suspect it could best be stated that Jung's followers suffer for lack of Freud and vice versa.

So much has been written about the relationship between Jung and Freud that there would be no point in my going into this area exhaustively, but there is one incident that has always seemed quite significant to me, which I've not seen mentioned anywhere. I learned of it in a conversation I had with Jung. It concerns the time after their break in 1913, when Freud, in his last effort to hold things together, had made Jung president of the First International

Psychoanalytic Congress. This didn't work, and Jung went back to Zürich very upset and distressed by the break. He began to try to pull together his ideas about the collective unconscious, which had ostensibly caused the break, or at least had been one of the principal breaking points between them. He had finally published this work in 1912 as *Wandlungen und Symbole der Libido*,[2] and sent a copy of it to Freud in Vienna. It came back by return post, with the pages uncut, and scrawled across the flyleaf was, *"Widerstand gegen den vater, S. Freud."* This means, "Resistance to the father." I asked Jung what he did then, and he said, "I turned to my wife, Emma, and I said, 'I feel as though I had been thrown out of my father's house'." (William McGuire, editor of the Freud/Jung letters, says he cannot trace this copy of the book to document my point, but if my memory is playing false, the essence of the story is true.)

I have always felt that this story expressed the heart of the matter—that the cause of the terrible feuding and fighting and bitterness that has gone on between Freudians and Jungians for so long was based on the unresolved transference-countertransference between these two men. And no wonder, their being two such titans!

My own focus has tended to be on the earlier part of Jung's work, which I find quite compatible with Frieda's and quite compatible with Erik's. It is worth mentioning that back around 1915 or 1916, Jung made the statement that the analyst was in a peculiar position because he found himself at the same time subject and object of the therapeutic process, and Frieda agreed with me that this was equivalent to Sullivan's formulation of the analyst as participant-observer. Also Jung's concern with ego development in the first half of life is very compatible with the whole trend of ego psychology, especially Erikson's, so I feel no conflict there at all. However, Jung's notions about the task of the second half of life are something else again; I'll go into these later.

---

2. First translated into English by Beatrice M. Hinkle, entitled *Psychology of the Unconscious*, and published in 1916 by Moffat Yard and Co., New York, and in 1917 by Kegan Paul, London. It was extensively revised in 1952 by Dr. Jung, translated into English by R. F. C. Hull, entitled *Symbols of Transformation*, and published in 1956 as CW 5.

Meeting Erik Erikson had a very profound effect upon me. When I first went to Zürich, I had an ego that was—well, to say that it was loosely put together would be enormously flattering. It was in about the same kind of shape as a dandelion that's gone to seed. If you went FWOOSH, it blew to the four quarters of the earth. And it's quite clear that at that stage in my career I couldn't possibly have withstood the then prevalent, very, very tough reductive analyses that were being dealt out by Freud and his followers in Vienna. I couldn't possibly have survived one. I remember hearing Erikson say years later, "You know, of course, that classical analysis, as it was conceived by Freud, is something that not everybody can withstand. You have to be a pretty tough-minded bird." My formulation for it was that you have to be awfully healthy to survive it. As Erikson said, there were a lot of people who got back to somewhere between nothing and five all right, but then they didn't return to age 71 or 43½ or 29½; they were still shuttling around all the way from San Francisco to Boston in a dazed kind of way. (I don't think he got overwhelming applause with that kind of comment, but this is a reasonable paraphrase.) It was clear I would not have been able to withstand that, and there were a lot of other people who wouldn't have either.

So Erikson's work on the identity problem was germane for me, because my precariously-put-together ego was really quite awkward, and I was perforce intensely interested in things that had to do with ego, ego integrity, and ego identity. (I might also say that Erik's article in the January 1956 edition of the *Journal of the American Psychoanalytic Association*,[3] on the problem of ego identity, is really a basic orientation point for student health and psychiatric services across the country. I have done a great deal of work in this field, and his formulations have been invaluable.)

Erikson has made some really important contributions to understanding youth with his ideas about identity crises and psychosocial moratoria. I have felt very strongly over the years that there is something in common between older people and college-age people—these are the two groups I most love to work with—and

---

3. Erik Homburger Erikson, "The Problem of Ego Identity," *Journal of the American Psychoanalytic Association,* Vol. 4:1, January 1956, pp. 56–121.

it is that both of these groups are free to move in almost any direction. The young people have not yet been identified by society, nor identified themselves as greengrocers or thieves or psychiatrists or any of those things, so they are free to move. On the other hand, people my age have shot their bolt—if you're not president of something-or-other by this time, it's just too bad, and you'd better write it off—and this gives them permission and freedom to go back and pick up stitches they might have dropped and to do all sorts of things that are quite exciting. Now that I've retired from my jobs at Cowell Hospital and the Psychology Department at the University of California and the Medical School too, I'm free to experiment with different things. A growing and serious passion for conchology is absorbing more and more of my time.

In this connection, I'm very interested to hear students say that they communicate better with the older members of the faculty; it's the younger ones they can't get through to and really communicate with. And it's interesting how often in families the fathers and the children are at odds, while the grandparents and grandchildren have a real rapport. In my case I didn't get along well with my parents nor with my children, but I did with my two granddaughters. What I've learned from working with students and young people in general isn't something I can sum up and write down, but my consciousness has been increased as a result of my interaction with them.

Frieda Fromm-Reichmann was also tremendously important to me as a person; she somehow gave me a feeling of being valid. I think I first got the nerve to speak to her because I was so struck by her pride in being a woman and in being Jewish. I went up to her and said this, and somehow we just started talking; I guess six or seven hours passed before we stopped.

There are many values she stood for that I found myself passionately in agreement with. Her statement that the goal of analysis is self-realization suited me very well indeed. I have felt strongly about this because I have seen about me a preponderance of people who seem to incline toward the notion that the purpose of analysis has rather more to do with adaptation. I'm not saying that I want to force everybody out of step with the collective, or that I hope they will throw up at dinner parties or anything awkward like that, but I do think this formulation of hers is very important.

Another of her ideas that interested me tremendously was her conception of "the drive toward health." This is one of the things I'm always reaching out for in my patients: their healthy side, in order to make some sort of working relationship with it. What impresses me in nature is that after you leave the rock kingdom and move on through the plant realm toward the amoebae and beyond, the one thing that seems to be most evident is growth. I don't suppose that old Mother West Wind cares very much whether it's good or bad—I suppose it's a matter of indifference to her—but I know that for me it is the real *raison d'être*. I think Frieda felt this very strongly, too.

One of Frieda's outstanding qualities was her extraordinary genius for meaningful relationships. She had the capacity for answering questions you didn't even know you were asking. To me her real genius and her real originality lay in this area. She told me that as time went on she did less and less interpretation with her patients, that she came more and more to feel that the crucial matter was the impact of one person upon another, the interaction. I must say I feel very much the same way.

# *Initii:*[4]
# *St. George*

## *Concepts*

I n attempting to condense Jung's psychological concepts, it
seems best to start with a description of the psyche as a whole
and then proceed to its various aspects from the outside
inward—that is, first those components concerned with relating to the outer world and then those having to do with relating to
the inner world.

In a general way the psyche is divided into two parts, the conscious and the unconscious. These two parts are unequal, the unconscious being by far the larger. There is no clear-cut demarca-
tion line between the two because things that are conscious one
moment may be unconscious the next. A common instance of this

---

4. Elements or first principles, sacred rites, sacred mysteries.

is the sudden inability to remember names when introductions are in order, names one knew perfectly well a moment before.

Jung defines consciousness as ". . . the relation of psychic contents to the *ego* . . . in so far as this relation is perceived as such by the ego."[5] That is, awareness of things does not *per se* represent consciousness. By way of example, I once had an older woman patient who had really been around. She had, as the saying goes, seen everything. But her experiences were all compartmented; they were not related to her ego. Thus while she was egotistical, her ego development was weak, and consequently she was extremely unconscious. People who have a developing consciousness are changed by their experience. She was relatively untouched. It was significant that in spite of a very sophisticated appearance, her handwriting was like that of a girl of fourteen. Actually, age fourteen was about the level of her ego development.

The unconscious is described by Jung as a ". . . psychological borderline concept, which covers all psychic contents or processes that are not conscious, i.e., not related to the *ego* . . . in any perceptible way."[6] The proof of the existence of the unconscious is mainly through the observation of its products. He subdivides the unconscious into two parts: the personal and the impersonal, or collective.

The personal unconscious contains repressed, suppressed, and forgotten contents—persons, places, things, situations—that have impinged on the individual since birth. Some of these contents are, *de novo,* emotional nodes, for example the father complex, the mother complex, or the aftermath of traumatic experiences. These nodes may attract related material and grow, as it were, by accretion; they possess the quality of drawing energy to themselves. Ultimately they may become complexes, sometimes powerful enough to threaten the ego, which is conceived of by Jung as the controlling complex of the individual and as existing partially in consciousness. Also present in the personal unconscious are many lesser complexes that lack sufficient emotional charge, energy, or

---

5. CW 6, par. 700.
6. CW 6, par. 837.

accreted material to disturb the balance of the individual.

The collective unconscious contains complexes that Jung calls archetypes. These are not developed by the individual; they are inborn. They consist of figures and motifs that have been oft repeated; that is, they have developed slowly during evolution and history. The motifs of these complexes are found in myths and legends which, although originating spontaneously in various parts of the world, show resemblances too striking to be coincidental. For example, the hero figure is one of the archetypes that lie in the collective unconscious of us all. Hercules, Siegfried, and St. George are representations of this archetype.

The night journey under the sea is a typical archetypal motif. For modern man this journey can be exemplified by analysis. Among the Navajo Indians this is still a living concept, and sick people are often taken through a ritual that recreates this theme. In our own heritage, the story of Jonah and the whale is a familiar example. Jonah was unable to speak with sufficient wisdom until he had made a journey under the sea, that is, until he had explored his unconscious.

This deep collective level is very much in evidence in childhood. The child, gradually and painfully emerging from this primordial matrix, slowly forges its ego by means of which the threat from the collective unconscious within can be held off. To accomplish this, the child must first identify with the mother and father in whom it is psychologically contained. As the ego becomes more clearly defined, the child continues to use the parents as protection against the outer world. One might add that the constantly developing personal unconscious serves as a buffer against the danger of the ego's being overwhelmed by the collective unconscious. However, night terrors frequently consist of archetypal material that is far too powerful for the child to deal with directly.

Jung speaks of the compensatory function of the unconscious, by which he means that an exaggerated attitude in the conscious will constellate its opposite in the unconscious. This depends on a theory of opposites based on the empirical postulate that each of us contains dichotomies such as goodness and badness, courage and cowardice, generosity and stinginess, love and hate, etc. Every

quality that exists in the conscious has its opposite in the unconscious. For instance, it is a commonplace that we repress feelings
of hostility toward those we love. But even without repression the
same rule holds. If we are good in one kind of activity, we tend to
be correspondingly inept in its opposite; that is, the opposite lies in
the unconscious and is relatively undeveloped. For example, a man
who is good at pure thinking tends to be all thumbs in human relationships, and vice versa. Thus it should be remembered that the
unconscious contains the positive and the negative, cheek by jowl,
and that what emerges from the unconscious depends largely on
our conscious attitudes.

Jung's concept of complexes is so important that it calls for
elaboration. He believes them to be formed by the combination of
a specific innate disposition and an outer event. They always con-
tain affect to a greater or lesser degree and grow by accretion.
They may be formed by a single event, e.g., a traumatic experience, or more often by a series of minor repeated incidents. They
may be helpful or harmful, positive or negative. It is only when
they acquire sufficient power to become autonomous, and thus
threaten ego-supremacy, that they become dangerous to the individual. They then behave like separate "I's," separate egos, and the
ego itself is forced into a subordinate role. In the old days, people
with this sort of psychic condition were said to be possessed.

In therapy it often seems unfruitful to make a head-on assault
on a complex, especially one that is of common occurrence. For
instance, it may be assumed that all men have mother complexes
and castration complexes but not necessarily ones that interfere
with their lives. To deal effectively with complexes that are troublesome, however, it is essential to establish a general attitude
apart from the attitude of the complex, that is, to strengthen the
ego point of view. The complex can then be brought into consciousness and assimilated. (This is notably difficult with schizo-
phrenics, whose ego structures are so weak that they are frag-
mented by the impact of archetypes, the inborn core of complexes, surging up from the collective unconscious.)

Jung speaks of the *shadow*—that side of the personality which
is unacceptable or infantile—as a complex. (As we all know, this

side not infrequently takes over!) He also regards our outer façade, or *persona,* as a complex, and this, too, sometimes blocks an individual's potential and stifles it. However, a persona that is under the control of the ego is often convenient and even essential. I could never survive a "tea-fight" or a society cocktail party unless I could hide behind the doctor persona. It is a great protection. So is the skiing persona at a resort, until one can get alone to relate to the mountains and snow in one's own way.

This concept of the persona—that is, the mask or façade—is familiar to everyone. It is the outer attitude, what one presents in given situations, one's adaptation.

Adaptation seems to be the *dernier cri* in this country, though it is by no means the hallmark of a well-integrated personality or of a true individual. With many people, it is compulsive and overwhelms them. They identify with a group, but as individuals they are *non est.* They do not know where the group leaves off and they begin. They are possessed by a societal persona. For example, some of us may have had the experience of arguing an Englishman into a tight corner and having him suddenly turn into the British Empire. He becomes impregnable and unassailable; everybody knows you can't lick the British Empire! Others identify with a parent, a teacher, or Babe Ruth, or with traditional roles such as the doctor, the clown, the tough newspaperman.

An amusing case of identification with a doctor persona came into my consulting room several years ago, via his wife. She sat down and said, "Well, we've come all the way across country for a vacation, but I don't care; I kicked him out of bed last night." I said, "Oh, did you? You mean your husband?" "Of course!" she replied, "What do you take me for?"

After a moment she simmered down and continued, "Well, I simply told him that I married a very attractive man twenty years ago, and if he ever came back, I would like to sleep with him again. But not with a doctor. Imagine being in bed with a doctor, even a good one!

"You see, as the years went by, he buried himself more and more in his medicine. His real nature began to get crowded out. It was 'the doctor' this, and 'the doctor' that. I even began calling him 'doctor' myself, so I suppose I aided and abetted it. And now he's disappeared altogether, and there's only a doctor left. I want to get back the man I love. He must be there somewhere!"

This is not meant to belittle the usefulness of the persona. Sometimes one suffers acutely from lack of persona. I started medical school relatively late in life, and I remember that when I was only about halfway through I visited a former college class-mate who was by then head of a big business. His desk was bris-tling with little boxes that all started to squawk urgent messages at him, and as I waited I began feeling more and more inferior. We were almost ten years out of college. Finally the messages stopped, and he swung around and said, "Well, well, so it's Jo Wheelwright. And what are you doing?" I had no persona to counter with. He had me.

During the process of growth, one needs identification; one's own ego is too imperfectly formed to withstand the outside im-pacts to which it is subjected. But as one matures, one disidentifies and merely uses the adaptations where they are appropriate. Thus, adaptation is hardly the aim of Jungian analysis. Too-good adapta-tion is always suspect; one wonders how much original individual-ity lies behind it. This is especially true in extraverted people, who tend to repress the subjective side and regard the outer world as the be-all and end-all of existence. Most of us are familiar with the pe-rennial sophomore. He has become identified with a persona that was appropriate in college. But in later life, it is at best amusing and at worst a downright headache. To the introvert, a persona is a life-saving device; to the extravert, there is a great temptation to *become* it. Outworn personae are faintly disturbing to other people. The right things are said, and yet they are not convincing. There is a flatness and two-dimensionality.

This somewhat derogatory treatment of the persona and the consequent whittling down of adaptation is not a brief for the phi-losophy that the world must adapt itself to the individual. It is only that Jungian analysis is concerned with psychological develop-ment. This means enlargement of consciousness and progressive disidentification with individuals, groups, and uncritically ac-cepted cultural attitudes and patterns. The ability to produce an

appropriate persona is important, but the real source of development lies within and not without. Potential must be raised from
the unconscious.

To increase consciousness, new material must be related to
the ego. The ego as defined by Jung is ". . . a complex of ideas
which constitutes the center of my field of consciousness and appears to possess a high degree of continuity and identity. Hence I
also speak of an *ego-complex.*"[7] He stresses the fact that he considers
the ego the center of consciousness but not the center of the whole
psyche. This latter center he calls the *self.*

The ego, then, is the boss complex, and upon its integrity and
strength depend the balance and effectiveness of the personality.
But the ego is running a three-ring circus, and its supremacy is
constantly being challenged. If any of the complexes gains a higher
charge of libido or energy than the ego, the ego is overwhelmed
until the complex has been depotentiated.

The first half of life is largely concerned with the ego's development and its struggle in the outer world. The ego is a composite
of inner and outer experiences consolidated by continuity and
memory. It represents one's own point of view, as apart from the
point of view of other persons, groups, or stylized roles.

Of course, it is not only external things with which we are
tempted to identify and to think of as synonymous with our egos.
Our ego identity is also threatened by inner things: complexes, archetypes, and the psychological functions of adaptation.

At one time I had a patient who was a professor in a women's
college. He saw nothing out of the way in Descartes's dictum, *"co-
gito, ergo sum"* ("I think, therefore I am"). Like Descartes, he was
identified with his thinking function; he thought that it represented
his ego. Being by nature a thinking type and thus uneasy in the
realm of human relationships, this man had decided he would have
to gain his security through intellectual competence. As time went
on, his neglected feeling function, his relating function, sank down
into the unconscious. And as he had shifted his conscious centrum
to his thinking function, there was no possibility for development

---

7. CW 6, par. 706.

except along thinking lines. However, thinking had become sterile for him; it was boring. Finally nature overthrew this unnatural dictatorship of thinking. He was overwhelmed with what H. L. Mencken described as "that intellectual catastrophe known as falling in love." This brought him to me.

It was striking how little ego this man had. He had nothing to which to relate his inner or outer experiences except his thinking function. So when his feeling function volcanically erupted—feeling being antipathetic to thinking, even incompatible with it at times—he was lost. In order for him to handle his feeling in this new development, it was necessary to help him rediscover his ego. He had to realize that thinking was only one tool by which his ego expressed itself and that there were other tools available to him.

Parenthetically, his case, as with most in my experience, clearly demonstrated the teleological nature of neurosis. Nature seems principally to be concerned with growth, and to achieve this end, she inflicts pain on her victims, those who falsify their true identities or fail to live up to their full capacities. Out of catastrophe comes new hope and new life. The phoenix-from-the-ashes motif nicely symbolizes a successful analysis.

The ego can also be dispossessed by projections from other people. A young woman patient of mine suffered from such a problem. No sooner would she get embarked on her own life course than a man would come along and fall in love with her. As a man has a habit of doing, he would project his inner feminine image on her and would have certain expectations of her. She would try to fulfill his needs, to enact the role, and in the process would become the *femme inspiratrice,* the inspiring woman. This was all very well for the man, but it kept interfering with her ego development. Because she was diffuse in relation to men—receptive, indefinite—it was natural that a man would make his own surmise as to her point of view, and she, being sensitive enough to catch on to what he wanted, would then assume that view and neglect her own potential.

A young analyst I knew in Europe fell into this trap with a Swiss patient of his. She was an extremely strong-willed and attractive woman. She overwhelmed men, and as she had very high

ideals and led an exemplary life, they were wont to see her as god-
dess. Now, it is hard for a young woman to be so idealized. It gets
boring and rather chilly standing at the top of a fifty-foot pedestal.
So, of course, in her unconscious she wanted some rough stuff;
she had a bit of the Clara Bow in her.

Her analysis seemed to be going along nicely. (This is the
time for an analyst to watch out; one tends to relax one's own consciousness, and then one is most vulnerable.) One night she had a
dream that shocked him into his senses and showed clearly that he
unconsciously had been acting out the masculine role that she unconsciously wanted for herself. She dreamed that he had small
horns and a pointed beard, unmistakably Mephistopheles. He was
striding up and down his consulting room, throwing her come-
hither glances and saying, "Let's go out together. The Waldhaus
Dolder is a nice hotel. Any night will do, any night." This jolted
the analyst back into his own point of view; his ego took over
again. For when he considered such a course of action consciously,
he knew he really had no desire for any such shenanigans, quite
apart from any moral and professional considerations. He liked
her, but not that much! So he had to explain his real point of view
to her and admit he had been guilty of leading her on, unconsciously to be sure; but most catastrophes in analysis occur
through just such lapses of consciousness on the part of the analyst. And dreams sometimes make useful objective comments that
nevertheless cause the analyst considerable discomfort.

A situation like the above probably would not have developed
on the basis of projection alone. Such projections are made because
there is a hook to hang them on. The young analyst was decent
and conscientious in his professional and everyday life, but he had
obviously made the mistake of thinking that this outer attitude
represented his whole point of view. As with all people who tend
to identify too strongly with goodness, badness was just around
the corner. Wherever there is a very pronounced conscious attitude, its opposite is bound to exist in the unconscious. To ignore
the existence of this opposite is to deliver oneself into its power.

Thus, the young woman's projection corresponded with a
concealed aspect of the analyst and activated it. This kind of unac-

ceptable aspect is what Jung calls the *shadow*. The shadow is what we apparently are not; it is the back side of the coin. It contains inferior—i.e., undeveloped—attitudes and functions, as well as infantilisms and other characteristics that are unacceptable to the ego and even more so, unacceptable to the persona. Some people identify with their shadows; their positive sides lie in the unconscious. In Switzerland, such people are called pitch-birds, a bird who always puts his foot in the dish. Although the manifestations of the shadow are always disturbing, unrealized values are also to be found in it. It is the gateway to the collective unconscious and may be considered a many-faceted complex. It is a complex that should be thoroughly explored in analysis. In large part its contents need to be brought into consciousness and assimilated. One might liken its relation to consciousness to the position of suppressed minorities in the body politic. If these minorities are excluded or ignored, they gain strength and ultimately threaten the going regime. In Russia they successfully upset the apple cart.

In other words, analysis insists that one's consciousness must be a democracy. One must acknowledge the existence of disparate psychological elements and give them their value. In a highly collectively-minded country like ours, there is a great danger of identifying with one's persona, one's adapted side, thus denying the existence of the shadow. This is precisely the situation that leads to a *bouleversement,* a reversal of the apparent personality.

Projection of the shadow onto other people prevents one from seeing one's own weaknesses and anti-social impulses. Jung once told me it was his impression that during the gangster era many Americans whitewashed themselves with the morning paper. They would read of the misdoings of Pretty Boy Floyd and Al Capone, click their tongues, and walk off to the office thinking, "What beastly cruel men!" And of course the unspoken corollary was, "What a fine decent fellow am I!" It was the scapegoat mechanism in action. In England everybody "knows" that the French are immoral and sexy. In France it is equally well "known" that the English are stuffy and unfeeling. Or so run the national stereotypes. In England, Americans are money-grubbers, while in America, Englishmen are snobs. And so it goes: shadow projections on a national scale.

The shadow is represented in dreams as a figure of the same
sex as the dreamer. Figures of the opposite sex, while they may
have some shadow characteristics, are, according to Jung, aspects
of the *animus* or *anima,* terms he uses to designate, respectively, the
masculine side of a woman and the feminine side of a man. The
genesis of these figures he ascribes to three factors: the biological,
the archetypal, and the environmental.[8] The combination of these
three factors forms a many-sided image of which we are relatively
unaware; that is, we are unaware of it as part of our psyche. We
say, "I admire such-and-such a type or such-and-such characteristics in the opposite sex." We remain in this blissful state of semi-
unconsciousness until we fall in love, at which point we become
almost completely unconscious. We have someone who appears to
correspond with our unconscious contra-sexual side. We project
the inner figure on the outer person, and the heavenly symphony
strikes up.

Lovers have extraordinary sensitivity to the desires of their
partners. They feel their way into the appropriate role, and as long
as each stays in character, they continue to move in celestial
spheres. This situation is easier to maintain in courtship, where the
pressure is not so unremitting. But in marriage the strain may become terrific. The demands of the animus or anima often become
too much for the partner to fulfill. Then one partner will be forced
into declaring his or her own point of view, which may have been
totally suppressed from consciousness. This is naturally a hard
shock for the other partner, who often comes back with an equally
out-of-role attitude. The disillusion in the face of these develop-
ments initiates a critical period; as the various aspects of the anima
and animus projections are peeled off, the partners are forced to see
each other as they really are.

At this point three directions are open. The two people concerned can gradually slip into a kind of marriage of convenience in
which there is scant personal interrelatedness. Often such marriages are maintained for the sake of the children, although, in fact,
children derive little security from such an artificial situation.

The second course, a regrettably popular one, is the old pil-

---

8. For fuller discussion, see Chapter III, page 37.

grimage through the divorce court. Like the first course, this often involves a lapse of consciousness, a regression. The partners let the animus or anima images, which can no longer be successfully projected, return to the unconscious whence they originated. This sets the stage for the same thing to happen again with a new partner.

The third course, which is to preserve the marriage—but not just as a conventional shell—is the most difficult one. It means working out a real relationship, pouring one's energy and passion into it, respecting each other's real nature. To do this, each must incorporate into consciousness the anima or animus aspects that had been projected onto the partner. Only then can one speak of real love.

To be harsh, the projection phenomenon with which most marriages start—being in love—is actually a kind of autoerotism. The magic quality comes from union with the unknown part of one's own psyche. It differs from a transference relationship with a psychotherapist only in that it is lived out in real life, while the transference experience is, or at least should be, "analyzed out" in an essentially impersonal framework.

The unprojected animus or anima produces certain definite effects when it is principally unconscious and unassimilated. In each sex it makes itself felt as an inferior representative of the opposite sex.

The anima, when it displaces the ego and gains the ascendancy, makes the man moody and emotional. He may be whiny, sulky, whimsical, passive, even bitchy and underhanded. This is, of course, its negative aspect. On the positive side it contains an eros quality and produces gentleness and sympathy.

One sees almost complete anima possession in certain male homosexuals, those who have strong compulsive mother ties. As with all men, their primary anima image has been the mother, but for them it has remained projected upon her. In these cases it is also usual for the mothers to be strongly son-fixated; they do not want to let the son escape. The unhappy victim is possessed by his mother who represents and is identical with his anima. He is not free to project other aspects of the anima onto a woman outside the family circle. His maleness is suppressed, and he has no possibility of identifying with the father or other male figures in order to build up his masculine side. As a rule one finds that the father is either a domineering stern fellow, who rebuffs the son's attempts to get close to him, or a weak man who possesses little maleness for the son to tie on to. Sometimes the father is dead or divorced, and there is literally only the mother in the boy's life.

The animus has certain characteristics. Negatively, it appears in the woman as opinionated, aggressive and domineering. It is always right; it must always win. It may think quite logically, but its premises are more than likely to be arbitrary and unsound. Every analyst knows how often one hears an animus-possessed woman make a flat, unsubstantiated statement and then proceed to build a case upon it. On the positive side, it gives the woman an independent, three-dimensional quality. If she runs the animus— rather than vice versa—it enables her to do creative, impersonal work, which is indispensable for a professional woman and, indeed, for women's individuation.

The animus and anima have important functions in the inner world as well as in the outer one. When properly integrated, they serve as liaison figures between the conscious and the collective unconscious. The poet's muse is a familiar example of this phenomenon.

Earlier I mentioned that during the first half of life the ego is concerned with the struggle for mastery in the outer world. During the second half of life there remains the task of exploring one's inner world. Jung has named this the *individuation process*. It is a process of expansion of consciousness, a pursuit that he considers the basic purpose of life. In the course of exploration of the inner world, one discovers the real center of the personality, the archetype that Jung calls the *self*. The Chinese concept of *Tao*, The Way, describes a similar process. True religious experience is involved, and it is largely because of his preoccupation with this realm of experience that Jung has frequently been accused of mysticism. The world of archetypes is a mysterious and unfamiliar territory, at least to the Western world. In the Orient, however, it is more familiar; there the American bathroom-and-plumbing preoccupation is the mystery.

## *Attitudes and Values*

SCREENING:

I suppose that one of the most important things I do as a therapist occurs before I do any therapy at all, namely screening. I consider myself really fortunate to have been able to pick and choose whom I work with. I haven't done this on an elitist basis; I've done it because of my own limitations. The very fact that I have certain gifts means the price of admission is that I have certain "ungifts." If somebody comes along who needs the kind of stuff I have only on my ungifted side, they'd be better off if they went to the movies. To me it's arrant nonsense to think that every therapist can be equally good with all kinds of people. I just don't think it's true.

So I usually have two or three preliminary interviews with prospective patients in order to give us a chance to size each other up, and unless all the little green lights go on inside my cranium, I suggest they go to one of my colleagues. For my part, I want to make sure in the first place that we can communicate, speak a language that seems to make sense to each other; in the second place, I want to make sure that there can be mutual trust; and in the third place, I want to be sure that I can actively believe in whomever I work with. I don't think it's enough just to accept people passively. I suppose if a one-legged, pea-green man came in and announced that he enjoyed cohabiting with sheep, I could probably sit there and not be too upset about it, even smile blandly at him. But it's got to be more than that; the person actually has to be important to me.

PATIENT FEES:

An interesting thing happened with Jung about prices. He said to me, "Now about charges . . ."
I said, "This is very embarassing, very awkward, because I . . . to tell you the truth, I am just about broke. We have been living in a basement on $150 a month for the last six years and my nest egg is pretty well dried up; there isn't much of it left."
"Well, I'll tell you what I'll do. In spite of that funny sort of British-sounding way you talk, you are an American, aren't you?"

"Yes, yes, it's just that I come from what I call the 'incest group' in Boston. (They all marry their cousins; it's the only place I know of outside of New Guinea where first-cousin marriages are not only permitted but even encouraged.) They all talk this way because they don't know they are Americans; they think they are British. I just never quite outgrew it." Jung thought that was pretty funny.

"Well, there are you are," he said, "you really are an American."

"Yes, I suppose I really am an American."

"Well, okay then, you're rich."

"I have just been telling you that I am not rich."

"Oh, everybody knows that all Americans are rich, so I tell you what. If you are a doctor, I will charge you half price. But I don't recognize all that M.R.C.S.L.R.C.P. stuff you talked about. What does all that mean?"

"Well, it's the equivalent of an M.D."

"I thought you were a doctor; I thought you had really done it. You said you were going to."

"Yes, I did it."

"Well, then you are a doctor, and so you get half-price. Instead of 15 francs, that makes it 7.50. Now, let me see, I'll just send you a bill every month. I know you can't pay me, but I want you to take it seriously. I don't want you to throw these bills away or burn them up or give them away to friends for souvenirs; they are real bills. What you do is take these bills and keep them and save them up. Then you pay me when you are rich the way all Americans are supposed to be."

"Okay, I'll pay you when I am rich."

I didn't feel that I was really rich enough to pay him until about the middle of the war, and I had a difficult time getting the money through to Switzerland, but I did. One of the first things I said to him when I saw him again in 1951 was, "I hope you got that money. It wasn't half enough, but I hope you got it." He laughed and said, "I told you that you would be rich someday."

That experience had a very profound effect on me because, of course, in psychoanalytic circles, a great deal is made of money. There is a great deal of what I consider hypocritical cant that goes

on about your analysis not doing you any good unless you fi-
nancially bleed and die, and therefore, "I am only charging you
this much for your own good, you know." Anyway, I think that
one's experience in analysis conditions a great many of the things
one later does as an analyst. I am sure this experience with Jung
had a lot to do with the fact that I have always seen many patients
for reduced fees or played "banker" for them. People say to me,
"But you can't do that; they will feel guilty and inhibited, and you
won't get a real analysis." It hasn't turned out that way. If patients
have problems about it, it is just grist for the mill, something more
to discuss. Actually, it has worked very well.

Jane and I settled something between ourselves at the beginning of our practices, and I am sure that it had something to do
with Jung's attitude. We decided to settle for making as much
money between the two of us as I could legitimately make by myself. This meant that we could take on many people who couldn't
begin to pay the going rates. In fact, I don't think we have ever
turned down patients because they couldn't afford it. This isn't intended as a boast about generosity. It is really selfishness in that it
has meant that we have been able to screen our patients and to
work only with those people we thought would find us meaningful and, because of our temperaments, more useful to them than
other equally good analysts down the street. So, it has been an in-
dulgence. We have made less money, but we have had very rich
professional lives. I attribute this largely to the attitude that Jung
had on this subject, and I must say that we have lived comfortably,
eaten and drunk well, and traveled widely. We have not been sac-
rificial lambs.

ANALYST-PATIENT RELATIONSHIP:

From the foregoing, it will be obvious that for me the interaction between myself and the patient is the crucial thing, and I
struggle hard to try and describe what in heaven's name it is that I
do. This is very difficult indeed, but one way I have of putting it is
that when I'm working with somebody, I hook one of my legs
very tightly around a leg of my chair, dispatch myself into the skin

of my patient, hang around in there for a while, pull myself back out again, and try to figure out what seemed to be going on while I was inside the patient's skin. That's one way I could say it. Or, I often think of it as plugging in with absolute concentration.

Something else that's important for me is to be no different in my consulting room from the way I am with my family or friends. Well, I don't make love to my patients, but I may laugh or cry, and I'm certainly more focused on the other person than I might be when I'm with a friend. I don't have the feeling of dispensing knowledge to swine who come in kissing my shoes. Nor do I use any sort of façade, any sort of technique. If ever I should, you can be absolutely certain I'm doing it not for the patient's sake but for my own, because I'm going down for the third time. That is, when I find myself falling back on technical devices, it is usually a defense to cover my own anxiety or feeling of inadequacy in the situation.

In other words, I've learned to treat therapy as a relationship, a process, and I try very hard to keep my theories out of this process because I don't want anything interfering with my immediate experience, my immediate contact with the patient. All that theory in my head isn't so important. Too much conscious concern with it tends to distort my observation and experience of the patient's quality. What is important—the indication of a successful therapy—is that both parties change, are touched by each other and grow.

DIAGNOSIS:

In the same vein, I would like to comment that I think diagnosis is a terribly dangerous thing. I'm enormously opposed to it in the field of therapy because if I start diagnosing people, all the things I've read about anxiety states, or hysterical conversions, or schizophrenia, or manic-depressives, or whatever it might be, immediately come flooding into my head. It's as if I'd pushed a button, and all this knowledge pours through the floodgates and gets between me and the person I'm working with. I used to say that before I'd start work with a patient, I'd rush in and grab an eraser off the blackboard and scrub my cortex absolutely clean, so there would be nothing preconceived between me and the patient.

I feel it is desirable to establish a relatively informal setting and to minimize the implications of authority inherent in the therapeutic situation. In this connection, I recall a day I spent with Jung in 1951 at his country place in Bollingen. It was the first time I'd got back to Switzerland since the war; I'd left in 1939, about 13 years earlier.

He said, "I hear that you are doing all right." I beamed from ear to ear, and then he added, "In spite of the fact that you are an M.D.!" What he was talking about was one of these archetypal things that we Jungians (including Jung himself) are enormously focused on: the whole tradition of the shaman, the healer, and the danger of identification with it. This happens when you think you're a cross between Mahatma Gandhi, Red Grange, Joe Namath and Siegfried: quite a galaxy of heroic material. I don't find this very good for the patients.

The hero archetype is a particular pitfall for me, and I think it is for many if not all psychiatrists. Mine took the form of St. George. When you're working with patients and realize that their needs and the place they're moving around in are very frightening and require a total mobilization of yourself in order to meet them and to accompany them and to match them, you often become not quite sure that you have it in you; maybe you could do it with about *that* much left over. It's a really scary thing. Well, at that point, sometimes I find myself being taken over by the St. George image. Mind you, I don't exactly look in the mirror and see myself in a suit of armor galloping across the fields after the dragon, but it gives me a kind of jolt; it's like a squirt of monkey glands. It gives me the ability to do a lot of things and to have all sorts of strength and courage that normally I don't have. But it is also a very fearsome thing; it's a little bit like putting a Porsche motor in a Volkswagen; you know, the chassis isn't quite up to it. So usually I have to go back and have another spin with my favorite analyst.

One thing that favors a reality-based relationship between analyst and patient, and implies rapport and reactivity on the part of the analyst, is more frequent use of the *vis-à-vis* arrangement as opposed to the couch. In London, the Jungians all seem to have slipped around the corner and bought a couch; but in this country and in Zürich, this is not so. I have bootlegged a couch, but I don't use it all that much, and my criteria for using it are certainly not the same criteria a psychoanalyst would have. I tend to use the couch when a patient has such verbal constipation that we both just sit there breathing for quite a long while. I think that is very expensive—after all, the patient is paying for the hour—and besides, it makes me feel very uncomfortable. A couch does help a bit, I think, in instances like that. But when I do use it, I'm likely to sit at right angles to the head of my patient, so that the patient can look at my beady eyes if he wants to, and if he doesn't want to, he can peer at the rubbing from Ankgor Wat, or he can peer at the wall. Not infrequently I will walk around the room; I've been described by one of my friends as a running analyst, in contrast to a sitting analyst.

The avoidance of anonymity seems to me to highlight one of the principal differences between the Freudian and Jungian schools. Jung has described the therapeutic relationship as an intensely personal one in an impersonal framework, personal but not intimate. It seems to me essential to establish a reality-based relationship concurrently with the transference-countertransference relationship. I am using the word *transference* to indicate projection of any unconscious contents. These include not only the unresolved infantile feelings and attitudes, but also contents that have remained *in potentia* and can only be assimilated into ego consciousness via the analyst. In my experience those things that need to be projected will be, without the therapist's forcing them by playing an anonymous role.

I feel that a large part of the effectiveness of therapy stems from reality-based interpersonal exchange between analysand and analyst. This means that the two people in the transaction are partners jointly engaged in a struggle to dispel the neurosis and explore the growth urge that afflicts the patient, including resolution of the transference. Therapy involves making an alliance with the healthy aspects of the patient, and until this has been accomplished, my primary focus is on health, not psychopathology. This is not an either/or, but a matter of emphasis.

An important implication of this approach is my belief that the healthy aspects need to be activated and encouraged throughout the therapeutic procedure. Erik Erikson once said that he thought one of the reasons Jung left Freud was that he could not bear Freud's unrelieved pessimism. While I recognize pain as a necessary concomitant of growth, it seems to me that neglect of the positive, healthy part of the patient overemphasizes the painful side of the procedure, even to the point of extolling it as a virtue. As the *reductio ad absurdum* of this tendency, I am reminded of the London navvies and charladies I used to treat during my medical training. Any attempt to give them palatable medicine was vigorously resisted; they used to insist on "the good stuff, Guv'nor, that nasty, 'orrid black medicine that mykes yer gag." In contrast to this and to balance the books, Frieda Fromm-Reichmann described her analysis as a joyous experience, and when I asked "You mean a liberation?", she agreed.

It seems to me important to hold theory in abeyance so nothing that can interfere with the immediacy of contact will stand between patient and therapist. An overly conscious concern with theory tends to distort one's observation and experience of the patient's quality. This attitude implies a minimizing of techniques. As I said, when I find myself falling back on technical devices, it is usually a defense to cover my own anxiety or inadequacy in the situation. But I am speaking only for myself, not prescribing the "right" way to do therapy. There is no "right" way to do therapy; each analyst must find his or her own style.

Jungians principally use dreams rather than free association to get access to unconscious material. Of course this emphasis brings up the question of attitude toward dreams. Does one take a dream as being in fact a distorted wish-fulfillment? If so, one is going to have to cope with the latent and the manifest content. Or does one only work on a dream reductively? Or does one, as I think Jung does, take a dream as a statement of how certain things are down in the basement at a given moment in time and space? Jung disbelieved in the idea that dreams are tailored by a censor and felt that if a dream was not understood, the failure was attributable to the analyst and the analysand.

In contrast to the systematic approach of Freudian analysis, which may be said to have a beginning, a middle and an end, the Jungian process is nonsystematic. A deep Jungian analysis is really a kind of controlled psychosis, a sort of guided tour through psychosis analogous to Virgil's trip with Dante. In other words, from the Jungian point of view, if you become psychotic, you're sloshing around in the primordial slime of the collective unconscious, rubbing shoulders with archetypes, and in a deep Jungian analysis, this is what happens. The nearest Jung came to formulating a system was when he made the statement that analysis consists of four stages: catharsis, explanation, education and transformation. But this is a general formulation and does not blueprint the clinical operation.

Finally, a basic Jungian attitude toward neurosis should be briefly stated: neurosis may be viewed as a challenge, an attempt by the organism to promote growth, as well as an illness. In short, neurosis has a purpose as well as a cause.

TRAINING ANALYSIS:

I think there are times when a man therapist is indicated and times when a woman therapist is indicated. I don't care how good a mummy I try to be, I'm just not as good a mummy as a woman is; and I don't care how good a daddy a woman is, she's not going to be as good a daddy as a man is. These are very arbitrary and provocative statements, perhaps, but that's the way it seems to me.

When I was first beginning to work with Jung, he said, "I suppose you're going to talk an awful lot about your mother. You've got the look of a mother-drowned man somehow."

I said, "Yes, I suppose so; yes, I expect so. In fact, I know of course I will; doesn't everyone?"

"No. And all that stuff just bores me to extinction. For forty years I've been listening to people talk about their mothers, and I can't stand any more of it. Now my assistant, Toni Wolff, tolerates it very well. So I tell you what you do: you go and talk about your mother to her. She will do very well with all that shadow business. Then when you have some archetypal material, something that's really interesting, we'll talk about that."

"Well, all right." I felt more than a little dubious about this arrangement, but actually it worked out very well. I saw Toni maybe three times a week and Jung once or twice a week. Curiously enough, there was remarkably little overlapping.

I've had my psyche tinkered with, I guess, by about seven different analysts since 1932, when I started down the road, and it's been about even, male and female. There's no question, as I see it, but that working with a female analyst activates things in my psyche—in everyone's psyche—that working with a man does not and vice versa; each activates, mobilizes, different aspects of the psyche. For just this reason, I have always been very keen on trainees being patients, somewhere along the line in their training, of both a man and a woman.

Another point about training is that in our Jungian training centers—and in the psychoanalytic centers as well—there is something that strikes me as awfully difficult and troublesome about the custom of casting the training analyst in the simultaneous roles of judge and therapist. To my mind these two roles are mutually exclusive, and this practice bothers me a great deal. If I could have my way about this, the training analyst would actually be disqualified from having anything to do with the promotion of the candidate.

I should also like to put in a plea for the encouragement of dissidence in the training centers and institutes. I find that things tend to move toward conformity, and in this way things tend to get crystallized into law and go dead.

Then, of course, there's the perennial chestnut which I think should be included in these remarks about the training situation. I will not be invidious about my colleagues, only about myself, in saying that when I was a young fellow, one didn't go into analysis only to get trained to be an analyst, at least this analyst didn't. I went because my psyche was in disrepair; I wanted and needed therapy. Most of us older people tend to react rather negatively when candidates present themselves and say, "Well, I'm perfectly willing to submit to analysis, you know; after all, I realize it's part of the training and everything; but of course I don't feel that I really need it." You can see the training analysts making black marks in their books about these people. But if a candidate comes in and says, "Of course what I'm really after is the therapy; I'm having some problems and difficulties, and after I've worked these through, I hope to become an analyst," then they're very tickled. It's rather tricky; one has to be neurotic enough, but not too neurotic. I don't know how this is going to develop, how it's going to be handled in the future. It's my impression that most of the candidates who are applying nowadays are in far less hot water than most of us were when we were young.

LAY ANALYSIS:

One thing that Jung and Freud did not disagree about was the question of lay analysis; they were both very strongly in favor of it. I happened to be having lunch with Anna Freud once, and I thought it would be interesting to hear her comments on the subject. So I said to her, "You know, Jung and Freud never thought about this, but what do you think about the M.D.s grasping psychoanalysis to their bosom and plunging down the football field with it?"

And she replied, "Well, your metaphors are a little peculiar. I don't really understand them quite, but I do get the gist of your question, and to tell you the truth, I am outraged by the whole idea."

"Oh, good! I know why I am; why are you?"

"Well, my father devised psychoanalysis as an investigative instrument. And those M.D.s, with all their therapeutic zeal, have perverted it almost beyond recognition." And then she went on to cite one of the reasons I'd also had for feeling the way I did about the importance of lay analysts: psychoanalysis and therapy in general simply can't be contained in the medical discipline, or in any one discipline, and they have suffered enormous deprivation from the loss of enrichment by anthropology, religion, philosophy, law and all the other areas that used to feed them.

# *Anima / Animus*

I think Jung's notions about the anima and animus are of great importance, and to introduce them further I would like to mention a little contretemps that took place between Erikson and myself. It came about one evening during World War II, following a psychiatric staff meeting at Mt. Zion Hospital in San Francisco, at which I was the only Jungian in attendance. The case of a WAC had been presented, and the ensuing discussion consisted very largely of ripples, in assorted pitches, of "penis-envy, penis-envy, penis-envy." After a bit I said to Erik, "Look, I think I get the general drift; let's just mosey along out of here." So we repaired to a nearby cafe where, over our favorite brew, the following exchange took place:

J.B.W.: "You know, we need some sort of grass-roots movement to counteract this situation, so I'm going to start a breast-envy club. I'll be president, and you may be vice-president."

E.E.:   "Good God, man, don't talk like that; you'll get into a homosexual panic!"

J.B.W.: "Well, maybe, but I don't feel it coming on me at the moment."

E.E.:   "You know, you Jungians are absolutely impossible, thanks to this notion of yours about contrasexual components. I think you get up every morning and water your anima or your animus, and you pat it and encourage it, and you think, 'Maybe someday I'll turn into an hermaphroditus.'"

I think this is a very fair statement of the Jungian attitude toward these contrasexual components.

The first of the three factors that combine to form the animus and the anima is the actual biologic slice of the opposite sex to which each of us is heir. The second and most important factor is the innate historical image of man or woman that originates in the collective unconscious and is as many-faceted as the traditional male and female roles. The animus contains such male incarnations as the hero, the villain, the romantic adventurer, the wise buffoon, the criminal, the father, the brother, the son. The anima contains a correspondingly infinite variety of female characterizations: the *femme inspiratrice* or inspiring woman, the hetaira, the Amazon, the imperious Lucrezia Borgia-like woman, the heroine, the mother, the sister, the daughter. Various aspects of these archetypal figures appear in myths and legends, which actually are the external record of the collective unconscious and are represented throughout the entire history of literature.

As a rule the way these things demonstrate themselves is, of course, by the projection route. I'm reminded of a really dramatic example where a man did a drawing that showed a woman in profile, chained to a rock face, her hands held out in a gesture of supplication. There was tremendous flooding and coming-down of water and lightning flashes. I asked him what it was, and he said, "That's a feeling." Then he paused, and said, "That's *my* feeling." Then he mentioned his wife.

Obviously there had been a very dramatic upheaval in this man's life. I asked him if he had ever heard of a lady called Andromeda. "She had a strong tie with Perseus," I said. "She was chained to a rock and in great danger. A monster was nibbling at her, and all this because her father was trying to get rid of her so that he wouldn't be displaced from the throne." I ran along through the myth to the point where Perseus does this magnificent business of dropping 390 feet vertically without breaking a leg. He scoops her up, breaks the chains, and off they go. Well, no, he hadn't ever heard of this; he hadn't ever heard of this at all. But yet there was for him a potency in this fantasy that was so overwhelming and so overpowering—this need to rescue the damsel in distress—that he had left his wife and family, after seventeen years of marriage and gone off with a young girl. And this young girl, his new wife, was very ready to act out the part. She had very little ego development, and the marriage went quite well, except that in order for him to do this kind of monkey business, it was necessary for this chap to be much, much more capable and competent than he really was. He had to be a kind of hero because this girl was pretty sick. So he had gone along being a hero for a bit, and then it had got to be too much for him, and he caved in and fell into a depression.

I have cited this case merely as an example of how this anima thing can work, not how it necessarily has to work. Hopefully one would be able to assimilate such an experience.

An American film of the 1940s, *The Affairs of Susan,* is an interesting study of a woman who acts out the anima projections of three different men. As the men discuss her, it develops that each perceives her in a different way. One sees her as a child of nature, another as an intellectual, the third as an incorrigible flirt. In actuality, as the audience has seen, she has behaved toward each exactly as he described her. In the end she refuses to play any role that falsifies her true nature and insists upon being accepted as she really is.

D. H. Lawrence writes of a mutual anima-animus projection in *The Man Who Died*. He fantasizes that Christ pushes aside the stones blocking his tomb and emerges to heal first his body and then his spirit. The real substance of this story concerns his ritual-istic union with a priestess of Isis. She sees him as the lost Osiris, and he sees her as the mysterious, spiritually pure woman through whom he can be made whole and be for the first time part of ordi-nary human life. In their relationship they both experience a fusion of the spirit and the flesh, a very high form of religious experience for which many of us strive. A child who symbolizes the fruit of their union is conceived, and at this point the experience is com-plete. It remains for each of them consciously to incorporate the animus and anima values they had projected on the other.

It is this kind of experience that is always to some degree im-plicit when any one of us falls in love. And we develop psycholog-ically just to the extent that we are able to assimilate the values we have projected onto the opposite sex. Actually, it is only through the process of projection that we are able to visualize these values at all, but unfortunately most of us are so enraptured by being in love that we cannot face foregoing the thrill of it. The process of mov-ing on into a conscious relationship with our partner, and re-absorbing the animus or the anima, seems like a cold and uninvit-ing prospect. Consequently, we are likely to try either to prolong the ecstasy of projection or to repeat it with another love object. This self-indulgent, non-progressive phase of being in love is basi-cally autoerotic. Nevertheless, it is an absolutely essential prelimi-nary to establishing a more advanced love relationship. This latter relationship demands an increase of consciousness in both partners in terms of recognizing animus or anima values as distinct from the actual personality of the partner.

Men and women closely identified with a social or cultural group may be able to disregard the subjective, individual aspects of marriage and to maintain their mutual projections with relative success. Such people seldom develop serious marriage problems as they are in a state of *participation mystique,* or oneness, with their social matrix and thus tend not to have individual problems. They are concerned with resisting consciousness rather than pursuing it.

A modern play dealing with projected animus figures is Eugene O'Neill's *Strange Interlude*. Here, Nina is portrayed in relationship with three men, each of whom is essential to her and each of whom is more or less an incarnation of a male stereotype: the husband as provider, the lover, and Charles as artistic and spiritual representative of the animus. The play, however, merely states the problem; Nina makes little effort to withdraw and assimilate her animus projections.

Scarlett O'Hara, the heroine of Margaret Mitchell's novel, *Gone with the Wind,* is an example of a woman possessed by the animus, frequently in a negative way. She attempts to project her animus first onto Ashley Wilkes, the gentle introvert, and then onto Rhett Butler, the tough extravert, but is unsuccessful both times; no ordinary mortal could fulfill the role she demands.

Liza, in Moss Hart's musical play *Lady in the Dark,* is another animus-possessed woman, but she comes to a happier end. She is able finally to project her animus onto a young man after two unsuccessful attempts with other men. This frees her from her self-imposed, pseudo-masculine identification and allows the emergence of her feminine side and her eros values. The conscious reintegration of her animus is left unresolved in the play, but one feels hopeful about her achieving it.

The third factor in the formation of the animus and anima is the impress of figures from the outer world: mother or father, Greta Garbo or Humphrey Bogart. (I sometimes feel that the American anima, insofar as it is derived from the outside, is composed of equal parts of Mom and Betty Grable.) The power of these outer elements in animus/anima formation varies directly with their correspondence to aspects of the inner archetypal image. Movie stars, fictional characters, historical or contemporary men and women are likely to represent our conscious ideals. This is because we fail to realize that our ideal images are in fact projected aspects of our own psyche, so we tend to describe them in terms of other people.

Of these outer figures the mother and father are most important and the earliest to appear in the psyche, as would be expected. Behind them lie the archetypal mother and father, but the first thing everyone has to work through is the actual flesh-and-blood relationship. To negotiate this process successfully, it is of course essential that the parents do their part. This means that they must not live their lives through their children but must keep their own relationship alive and fulfill themselves in all areas of their lives. It is a truism, but an important one, that a good relationship between the parents is the best insurance for good psychological health in the children.

The animus/anima phenomenon seems to me to constitute one of the gravest American problems. Until 1939 England and the Continent were under the aegis of the male. There was an unbroken historical background for this pattern. If a husband and wife got into a fight, and the man was hard pressed—as he always can be when dealing with a woman whose career is relationship—he could retire into his archetypal role and become *the man,* identified with this stylized role for which there was so strong a precedent. He then became a superior, impersonal, unassailable figure, and there was nothing for the woman to do but submit.

But in the United States—and I found a similar condition in the U.S.S.R.—there was a new danger and a new hope. There was to be equality between the sexes. This held great promise, but like all important shifts it was bound to swing beyond the midpoint. Some two-thirds of our country's wealth was in the hands of women, and in less tangible ways they had increasing power. We may not have been as much a matriarchy as Europeans like to believe, but there was no denying that momism was rampant. This meant that in many areas of life the animus was in the saddle. The women carried the national sanction, and the men by and large were on the defensive. Of course, the men were aiding and abetting this situation. They tended to be passive with their women, to placate them with furs, jewelry, and other oddments. They dodged relationships with their wives either by insisting that the wives mother them or by burying themselves more and more in their businesses and professions. At parties they tended to congregate around the fireplace for a dirty story session, and the women had to all but undress and roll on the floor in order to break them up. Some Frenchman said, "All generalizations are false, especially this one." Perhaps such a leaven is needed for the foregoing statements, though they cannot be dismissed as mere assumptions.

With this preamble I shall attempt to describe the pathological development of the animus and anima in relation to the mother and father, first in reaction to a dominant mother and a weak father, then in reaction to a dominant father and a weak mother. The description must be further subdivided into the two kinds of negative animus and anima behavior: that directed inward against the subject and that directed outward against other people.

In those families where the mother is dominant, she is almost always an animus-possessed woman and the father an anima-possessed man. As we all know, these types have a strong affinity for each other and are often found worrying through life together. In such a situation the growing daughter has no satisfactory man on whom to project her animus. Worse yet she is up against her mother's animus. In order to survive she is forced either into open competition with the mother or into a kind of underground passive-resistance campaign. In either case abnormal animus development is fostered in the growing girl.

Jill was a girl who took the underground course. The only authority she knew was the pseudo-masculine animus of her mother, and this was the only criterion she had for her development. Outwardly she appeared passive and submissive, but inside she was in constant ferment. Because she adopted her mother's attitude of contempt for men and her mother's view that the world's work had to be done by women, she began imposing impossibly high standards on herself, thus falling victim to the characteristic perfectionism of a negative animus. Inevitably, she failed to attain those self-imposed standards, and was, in fact, constantly undermining herself from within while her mother was undermining her from without.

Eventually her life goal began to come clear: to do some one thing better than anything her mother could do. Toward this end she chose woodcarving for which she had some talent and which provided her a relatively safe means of indirect competition. Having no interest in woodcarving, the mother did not feel her supremacy was being threatened, and she made no attempt to block her daughter's effort in this enterprise. The young woman's determination to outdo her mother was a closely guarded secret, necessarily so since she feared her mother and was unable to meet her head-on. But in the end she even blocked herself in this maneuver, since she was unable to perform as well as her animus told her she should.

Instead of identifying with her mother, she identified with her henpecked father. Before long it was apparent that he had projected his anima upon her and that she was acting out the role, thus stifling her own individual development. Ultimately her life arrived at a complete standstill, and she came for analysis.

Lena also had a dominant mother, but her reaction was the opposite of the above case. She developed an out-hitting animus and openly fought the mother. Her determination to win expressed itself in all her activities. She excelled in athletics and was a leader in all school affairs. Later she became an ardent feminist and joined a radical movement. Her relation to men was that of a companion and equal. She could think as well as they did and do all the things they did. It was frequently said of her that she thought like a man. Increasingly, her one purpose became to do her mother in, and her whole life began to revolve around this. When her mother forbade her to go to New York and refused to give her the necessary money, she promptly announced that she would go regardless and earn her own way. This terrified the mother who capitulated and supplied the funds.

In love relationships, Lena was shy and inexperienced on the eros, feminine side. But her animus, like her mother's, was constantly scheming for supremacy. Her sexuality was compartmented like a man's; her feeling was so deeply repressed that her sexuality split off from it. She had read numerous psychological books and concluded that "free love," as it was called in her day, was the answer for her. Nevertheless, she eventually married an anima-possessed man, passive and dependent, and after several stormy years divorced him. Like the woman in the preceding case, there was no feminine principle with which she could identify, as this side of the mother was so very undeveloped.

Nancy had a weak, helpless mother and an overbearing father. It was easy for her to project her animus onto the father, but in this case it boomeranged. By virtue of the projected animus, she endowed him with the power to destroy her, and this he very nearly did by his rigid ideas about how she should behave. For a while she was able to fulfill his expectations, but only at the expense of her own natural development. At this stage she appeared to be provocative and fascinating. By the time she got to college, however, her real nature began to emerge into consciousness. Her first response was to rebel, but she lacked the strength to accomplish this successfully. The result was a deep split between what she actually was and what she and her father had thought her to be. Her animus, which embodied the opinions of the father, attacked her remorselessly. It was a long and painful process in analysis for her to consolidate her ego and relate her animus to it.

Joy also found it easy to project her animus onto her powerful father. Her mother she felt to be of no account; feminine women were weak, foolish creatures. She was like her father, strong and fearless. This he liked and encouraged, for he had always wanted a son. His anima being safely projected upon his wife, he encouraged Joy's identification with him via her animus. Of course they sometimes had fights—loud, boisterous affairs—but in the end they always made up. She simply ignored her mother and other women unless they served her purpose; if they attempted to cross her, she rode roughshod over them. Men she treated in the same high-handed manner. However, she married, and it was from her husband—a quiet, unassuming man whom she always undervalued—that she finally got her "comeuppance." One day he simply announced that he was sick of being married to an arrogant pseudo-man, that he was going to get a divorce and find a real woman for a wife. This left her feeling utterly defeated, and it almost killed her because one of the hallmarks of the negative animus is that it must always win. But the blow had stunned the animus so that her feminine side could be reached in analysis and strengthened sufficiently to push the animus out of the saddle.

So much for abnormal animus development. The development of a man's anima is also governed by the psychology of the parents and their relation to each other. It should be remembered that for normal development the growing boy needs to be able to identify with the father, assuming that he is secure in his own maleness. The boy also needs to be able to project his anima onto the mother, a process that she should neither deny nor take advantage of. As he goes through adolescence, the other aspects of his anima will emerge and be projected upon girls his own age outside the family circle. His mother will gradually disengage herself from his primary projection onto her and leave him free to develop his life apart from her.

However, it is pathological development that I am engaged in describing here. First I shall describe a case in which the anima is directed against the subject in reaction to a dominating mother. Ned had an outgoing, warm mother. She adored him as a boy and encouraged his identification with her. The father was a friendly but passive man, occupying a vague and shadowy position in his son's consciousness. The boy showed definite signs of becoming homosexual. Fortunately, however, he was popular at school and able to make identifications with several of the teachers and students. While this helped him to fight the mother, she, who was identical with his anima, subtly depreciated his attempts to establish his masculinity, with the effect of dinging his rebellion so as to render it self-destructive. An older brother, who might have been an ally, sneeringly rejected him, thus reinforcing the self-immolation.

The boy defied the mother obliquely, for instance by refusing to apply himself to studying the piano, which in fact he passionately loved. This nicely upset the musical mother, but it also hurt him. Later he became an alcoholic, and again he was successful in distressing the mother, but this time he also wrecked his college career and damaged his own health in the process. His relationships with girls were on a mother basis; he was very passive with them and invited attack, then frustrated them beyond words by agreeing that he was no good. This fixed them, the mother surrogates, very nicely, but like all his machinations it fixed him too. Finally his physical resistance became very low, and he contracted pulmonary tuberculosis. The consequent period of enforced introversion in a sanitorium gave him the opportunity to acquire some insight, and he determined to tackle his problem analytically.

In this next case, Robert, in contrast to Ned, developed an aggressive anima in reaction to his mother's power. Early on he recognized his father's inability to cope with his mother's assertiveness and resolved that he, the son, would fight back. However, getting no masculine support, he used the weapon against which his mother was least able to defend herself, the bitchy side of his anima. This resulted in a really bizarre situation: when she bore down like a tyrannous man, he lashed back like a vengeful woman, hitting at her weak feminine side. Things finally came to such a pass that he produced a similar mechanism whenever he was opposed by anyone, and in spite of his brilliant mind ended up alienating people. By the time he sought analytical help, his job was in jeopardy, and he had become very isolated socially.

In the following case a negative anima is directed inward in reaction to a weak mother and overly dominant father. Barry said that ever since he could remember, his father had bossed him, criticized him, rejected him. His mother suffered a like fate, and she and he became close companions in misery, fellow-martyrs. His anima caused him to behave as his mother did; he was in the habit of complaining about how unable he was to cope with the inexorable rightness of the father and how he felt like a frail reed, unworthy, and a burden to everyone. At this point, of course, his listeners were supposed to respond, "O, no, not at all. It is really you who are good and Christian, and your father is a cruel tyrant."

This attitude was a subtle revenge on the father, who became doubly primitive when he was thus branded as the family stinker. However, the boy eventually overplayed his hand; friends and relatives got tired of bolstering him up and began to take him at his word, tacitly agreeing, as he was always insisting, that he was no good. This left him hurt and bewildered. It was interesting that the one who brought him to analysis for help was the cruel father.

The last of this series is the case of Larry, whose negative anima was directed outward in reaction to the same type of parental setup as in the foregoing case. This father was a stern Puritan identified with the spare-the-rod-and-spoil-the-child maxim. The son was unable to identify with him and unable to compete with him. He developed an abhorrence of authority and became prickly and catlike with other men. He liked to have his own way and if thwarted by authority lashed out in an emotional, underhanded way. Like many in his predicament, he found it easier to associate with women from whom he felt no threat of authority. To them he was able to relate as friends, whereas with men he was tense and ready to strike out if crossed. This wariness toward men, an attribute of this man's aggressive anima, is frequently characteristic of aggressive women. It was his repeated clashes with authority on the job that finally forced him into analysis to seek a solution to his problem.

Although I have discussed the negative animus and anima, both passive and active, in terms of their developing solely in reaction to the parental influence, my actual clinical experience leads me to believe that these are probably inborn tendencies. However, environmental influences do seem to have an exacerbating effect. Of course, the cases presented above are greatly over-simplified in order to highlight more graphically the animus and anima mechanisms. Actually, the animus and anima are strongly colored by other psychic contents, such as the undeveloped functions (as might be inferred from the preponderance of marriages that are polar-opposite in terms of psychological type). They are also contaminated by other elements of the shadow. For example, a somber man's anima is likely to be joyful, and a flighty woman's animus is probably solid. In dream material during the early stages of analysis, the figures representing the shadow are very often married to animus or anima figures. This combination makes a formidable bloc for the ego to deal with.

Perhaps the best way to summarize the roles of the animus and the anima would be to present a sketch of the history of a man and woman through a critical early marriage and on into a full, stable relationship. The woman's childhood had been a vexed one. She grew up in a small isolated community where the constant, enforced, close contact with her mother resulted in an ongoing battle royal between them that lasted for many years. The mother was an intellectual, very poor at domestic life, a typical animus-possessed woman, opinionated, hysterical when trapped, always arguing to win, and so extraverted that she had little respect for the subjective side of life that was of such importance to her daughter. She would worm confidences out of the girl only to use them against her in winning an argument, with no regard for their intrinsic validity. On the positive side it should be said that she was brilliant and witty with aspects that were gay, adventurous, and attractive, but it was not until much later in life that her daughter was able to appreciate her.

The father played a minor role. Gentle and passive, his achievement was powered by his wife's animus. It was said that he didn't know he had any children. When they were away in boarding school, he wrote them only one letter. The daughter was a little puzzled to get a letter that began "Dear Son," until she compared notes with her four brothers and found he had written the same letter to all of them via carbon copies.

Against this background the girl became reticent and secretive. Not being as quick as her mother, she had to do things that were rebellious. She became coldbloodedly determined to have her own way, to refuse to give in, to develop independence and self-reliance. These traits are animus attributes that are all right up to a point, but in her they were so exaggerated that they stole the libido from her feminine side. The only eros quality left was sexuality, and this was largely as a reaction against her mother's puritanical repression. She married a man somewhat like her father, though less practical and more imaginative. He was drawn to her unconsciously as a strong mother who could help him realize his potentialities. The conscious reason for their marriage was to legalize their sexuality. She insisted it be taken in that light, and he, wanting her badly enough, agreed and tried to suppress his feeling. There was no church wedding, no honeymoon; she would actually rather have maintained their secret alliance—more modern and feminist, her animus said. However, he persuaded her that the game of hide-and-seek wasted too much time and energy. So she married him but insisted on keeping her maiden name. Once she was a wife she felt trapped; the very word *wife* was taboo. Her husband tried to achieve peace at any price, but she bossed him, criticized him, tried to reduce everything to fundamentals. Their roles were actually reversed, she doing the thinking and taking the initiative, he pouring all his strength into holding the relationship together.

After several years of continual internecine warfare he became resentful, whiny, defeatist. By this time they were in their thirties, three children had been born, and they felt that they must work it out somehow. Emotionally exhausted and desperate, they both turned to analysis for help and began to discover their shadows. She had a dream representing this in which she saw the wall of a tenement building falling down, disclosing misery, poverty and grime. He had a vivid fantasy in which, instead of letting her carry him, as was the case in real life, he was carrying her. Weary months followed during which each brought into consciousness a considerable amount of unpalatable shadow material. Gradually the situation improved. He trained himself for a teaching career, knowing for the first time in his life what he really wanted to do and was fitted for. She handled the children better, and they responded by becoming happier and more relaxed. She even managed to squeeze in some professional training for herself without competing with her husband.

And then the wife developed an overpowering transference to her analyst. With his help she was able to understand and integrate the experience of the animus for which he was a focus in a truly definitive way. Several dreams are pertinent here. In one she dreamed that she was a young girl walking in the woods with her father and that she was his mistress. Her father, of so little importance in her conscious life, had become all-important in her unconscious. His suppressed eros side—not only sexual, but in a far broader sense—had been relegated to her unconscious and was united with all that she had repressed in herself. Bound to her father, she had been unable to make a full relationship with a man of her own generation. Later she dreamed:

> X (the analyst) and I are sitting at a table in the courtyard of an inn. We eat and talk. After the meal we get up and say goodbye. There is sadness but no regret, and we both know it is final. I must go to my fourth child (she had only three in real life), a young illegitimate boy.

This is a transformation dream; her experience with the analyst came to an end, and they parted on good terms. The fourth child represented the psychological product of their work together; he was the new development, the new value, she had gained. By now she had moved back wholeheartedly into her marriage. Soon afterward she had the following dream:

*I am at a large party. There are many people—some familiar, some unfamiliar, some distinguished, some not. My analyst steps out of the crowd and asks me to come with him; he wants me to meet a very important person. He leads me to my husband, smiles, and disappears.*

This dream represented more or less the completion of her transformation. Not too surprisingly her husband had become hurt and resentful because of her intense transference. Emotionally vulnerable, he developed a roving eye and half-consciously looking for trouble, found it: he fell in love with another woman. Having enough insight to realize that he must take the affair as an anima experience to be worked through, he sweated over his unconscious material, and with his analyst's help, he was able to detach his anima projection and relate it to his ego. He finally came back into the marriage more truly male than he had ever been, no longer possessed by his anima, which now served him as a relating function in his outer life and as a connection with his inner life, the deeper creative layers of the unconscious.

The wife, too, was relating properly to her inner figure, the animus. Although an introvert—an especially difficult attitude type for a woman in this country—she had developed her extraverted side sufficiently to enable her to handle the outer demands on her time and energy. At the same time she remained aware of her introversion and related to it through the animus, which was strong but most of the time her servant rather than her master. Able to use it productively in her profession of teaching and research, she was then left free to live her eros side in relation to her husband and children. Their roles were no longer upside down; he now was really the man and she the woman. This all happened many years ago, and they have since had an extremely good and meaningful marriage.

I must say in conclusion that this case is not intended as a brief for extramarital affairs. It was an exaggerated and ticklish business and was chosen for this discussion only because it illustrates so dramatically the anima-animus problem in relation to a successful marriage. It was little short of miraculous that one or the other of them did not fall by the wayside.

# *Psychological Types*[9]

I'd like to start off by saying that *types* is really where I came in on the Jungian scene. It happened after those three years or so during which my wife and I had been moving around the world, living out of suitcases and very much cheek-by-jowl. While there were lots of good times, there were also times when it seemed as though the other one was actually being difficult on purpose. I often had the feeling that it was as George Bernard Shaw once said about the English and the Americans: we were two people divided by a common language—a language that produced a great deal of stereotypy and a great many erroneous assumptions.

---

9. Previously published in a slightly different version by the C. G. Jung Institute of San Francisco, © 1973.

When we arrived in Zürich, one of the first things that was put into my hands, by Cary Baynes, was a copy of Jung's *Psychological Types*.[10] This book was a tremendously enlightening experience for both of us. It helped us to begin to see why we were having the kinds of misunderstandings we were. We suddenly discovered that I had a developed feeling function, and she had a developed thinking function. Of course this was upside down; everyone over the age of nine knows that men think and women feel, though it didn't seem to be that way in our family. So now we had some illuminating concepts to work with. After forty-two years there are probably still a few wrinkles left in our marriage, but the conflicts around type considerations are no longer quite as flamboyant or momentous as they were in those early days. No doubt this is due in part to the fact that both of us have done a lot of homework. Also, both of us are very much committed to the whole business of growth and development, of change and realizing potential rather than *status quo*.

There is a little story about types that I'd like to insert here. My friend Gregory Bateson, an anthropologist and creator of the "double bind" formulation, decided one day that he was getting rather old to be paddling up and down the rivers of Papua. He decided he would "psych the psychs" instead, so he went to work and did a field study on us at Langley Porter Clinic. He came up to me and said, "Jo, what's all this about types? I keep hearing you talking about this stuff, and I hate putting people in boxes." And I replied, "Well, Gregory, the most important thing about types is detyping." "Oh," he said, "I like that very much," and he wrote it down in his little book.

I also can't resist, at this juncture, putting in a couple of quotes from a poem that was written by Leonard Bacon. Bacon died some years ago; he had been one of the editors of the *Saturday Review of Literature*. He went out and had his psyche tinkered with by Jung and Toni Wolff in the early twenties. He wrote a Jungian alphabet, which included among other things, "E is for Extravert, finest that lives/Whom the Introvert never forgets nor forgives."

---

10. CW6.

And, "I is for Introvert, taking a ride/In a squirrel-cage hung in his little inside."

It is of interest that Jung worked out his type formulations as part of his lifelong attempt to understand what went wrong between him and Freud. I'll come back to this later on, but not everybody is aware of the fact that this is what really propelled him into these formulations.

For people who tend not to correspond to a cultural stereotype, I think that types are, willy-nilly, of great importance. One of the things that I have liked about types—apart from the fact that they were of such importance to my wife and me—is that types cut across party lines. I've talked to quite a few psychoanalytic groups about types, and nobody has to get into terrible theoretical agony about it, because there really isn't much conflict. Another thing that is noteworthy about types is that they are based on what one would hesitantly call "normality," if there is such a thing. All of us psychiatrists are dubious about that, but at any rate, Jung used to say that one of his greatest debts to Freud was that Freud and his followers had gone so thoroughly into psychopathology that it had left him free to explore the healthy aspects of the psyche. Consequently, most of Jung's terminology is based on notions of health, as opposed to Freud's terminology, most of which is based on pathology. Erikson, another man who has extended Freud's work, also has concentrated on the healthy and developmental aspects of the psyche and has created his own vocabulary.

Before I start to describe the types, there are a few things I might just mention. First, there are a couple of novels which, without it being explicitly stated, are based on Jung's types. One of them is *The Sign of Jonah,* written by a woman named Nancy Hale. She worked for a long time with Beatrice Hinkle, a Jungian analyst in New York, and is very knowledgeable about Jung's work. The other one that occurs to me is by C. S. Lewis, the *Screwtape Letters* man; it's one of those science-fiction books and is called *Out of the Silent Planet.* It describes four cultures, each representing one of the four functions.

I also want to speak briefly about the type test that Horace Gray, my wife Jane, and I developed. It is enormously helpful to a therapist to be able to estimate the abilities and limitations of patients in terms of their possible behavior and adaptation. And it's essential for the therapist to explain things to patients in a language they understand. To talk intuitively to a fact-oriented man or intellectually to a woman who lives through feeling can be a waste of breath, as well as a frustration to the patient.

So the three of us spent a very long time during World War II working out a type test. We occasionally involved Joe Henderson in our struggles. Gray and I were a perfect team for the job because I was an extraverted intuitive-feeling type, and he was an introverted sensation-thinking type, as was Jane. We figured that between us we added up to one, and we ought to be able to do it. So we sat around dreaming up questions. Based on the premise that charity begins at home, the first questions arose from our own conditions, as it were. They were then subjected to all kinds of testing-out on people whose type had already been clinically identified. Horace, who was a good mathematician, had stumbled on something that scientists seem to think a great deal of: the *chi-square*. This always made me very nervous; I don't know what *chi-square* means, and I'm determined that I never shall know. But he used it all the time, which apparently made the questions quite respectable.

Many vexed marriage situations revolve around this business of types. My research with Gray showed that in a sample of over a thousand subjects, the overwhelming majority had married their polar-opposite types. On the other hand, they tended to pick for friends types similar to themselves. I wanted to include the comment that the obvious conclusion was that people marry people they wouldn't dream of having as friends, but Gray was a very dignified man and wouldn't let me do it.

Of course, at first it's very impressive to find that one's spouse can do what one cannot do oneself. It makes one feel completed. But then there comes a time when one or the other partner gets weary of carrying the other one's load. Now if the two partners can really accept the fact that in their type difference lies their original fascination with one another, as well as their present disenchantment, this could be a turning point in their marriage, *if* they're willing to develop their inferior sides.

Jung's idea of individuation is closely related to types. As long as we are content to let somebody else carry our introverted side, or our feeling or another function, we remain relatively unconscious and undeveloped. Of course, Jung felt that growth involves a constant increase of consciousness—that is, the incorporation into our conscious personality of aspects of our psyche that have hitherto lain in the unconscious. This shift is usually carried out by projections onto others that are identified as such, as in the analysis of the transference. Actually, in the marriage situations usually one or the other of the partners goes on strike. After two years, five years, ten years, one of the partners says, "That's enough of that stuff. I'm perfectly willing to think for myself, but I'm not going to think for two." Or, "Why don't you do your own feeling from here on." C. A. Meier delivered a paper entitled, "Psychological Types and Individuation"[11] at a Jungian Congress. In this, he gave several case histories describing the relationship between the emergence of the inferior function and the whole individuation process. (*Individuation* is a word that makes me rather nervous. I prefer to stick to the homely word *growth*.)

Katherine Bradway and Wayne Detloff have done a piece of research using our type surveys, and they found something striking. What they came up with was that the Jungians in San Francisco and the Jungians in Los Angeles came out 90 percent introverted and 80 percent intuitive—rather high ratings.[12] I'm abso-

---

11. C. A. Meier, "Psychological Types and Individuation: a Plea for a More Scientific Approach in Jungian Psychology," in J. B. Wheelwright, ed., *The Analytic Process: Aims, Analysis, Training*, Proceedings of the Fourth International Congress for Analytical Psychology. New York: G. P. Putnam's Sons for the C. G. Jung Foundation for Analytical Psychology, 1971, pp. 276–89.

12. K. Bradway and W. K. Detloff, "Psychological Types and Their Relationship to the Practice of Analytical Psychology," *Professional Reports, Second Annual Conference of Jungian Analysts of Northern and Southern California, the New York Association for Analytical Psychology, and Individual Members of the International Association for Analytical Psychology Residing in the United States*. San Francisco: C. G. Jung Institute of San Francisco, 1975, pp. 29–53.

lutely convinced, because I've spent a lot of time in psychoanalytic circles, that the opposite is true in the Freudian scene, that their members are predominantly (I would guess about 80 percent) extraverted and sensation types. They're very consistent in these two aspects. Jung had arrived at a similar conclusion with regard to himself and Freud; namely that Freud was heavily weighted on extraversion and sensation and he on introversion and intuition. (It is interesting to note that the picture is changing in the San Francisco training program. Six extraverts were admitted to candidacy in 1976.)

One thing that has been extremely noticeable in connection with the emphasis of Jungians on introversion and of Freudians on extraversion is reflected in the establishment of training centers. Freudian training centers got under way very early. I don't know exactly when the first one in the United States (it was in New York) opened its doors, but it was sometime in the early twenties, and the Boston one got going about forty years ago. Of course, the very first one was founded in 1911 in Vienna with Jung as president; Freud was making a last effort at trying to hold things together between them. In England, Jones and Glover got Freudian training centers started quite early on.

Among Jungians it has been quite a different sort of thing. I recall that in 1939, when I was about to leave Switzerland to come back to America, I asked Jung, "Couldn't you perhaps jot down a few criteria for trainees? We really ought to have some sort of standards."

"Oh," he said, "I'm writing a book, and I have got some dream material I'm working on. No, to tell you the truth, I really just can't. Why don't you do it?"

"Well, you know, I'm a beginner, and I'm absolutely terrified. I couldn't possibly do it, and nobody will pay any attention to me anyway."

"Well, you're extraverted. You go ahead!"

Actually, when I got back to America, my wife Jane, Elizabeth Whitney, Lucile Elliott, and I did get something started; soon Joe Henderson joined us from New York. We pushed and pulled and struggled, and we eventually did get a real training center established by 1944. Then, in 1951—which was the first time in twelve years that I'd got back to Zürich—I went out to Bollingen to spend the day with Jung. I said to him, "You know, Dr. Jung, I did it!"

"Really? What is it you did?"

"That training center we were talking about in 1939. Well, we had a lot of help, of course, but it's going, it's going! We have lots of candidates—two—and we have five card-bearing members; it's really . . ."

Then I saw he had a faraway look, as though he'd moved off, and I said, "Well, I can see you're not very fascinated."

"No, to tell you the truth, I am not very fascinated. There's really nothing I would less rather talk about." (Up to then I had been full of enthusiasm, but this did dampen me a bit.) "Well, that isn't very nice of me. I see you're quite upset, and I suppose you must have some sort of an organization. Why don't you try and have the most disorganized organization you can manage?"

"Oh, we have, Dr. Jung! We have!"

Something else I'd like to mention in passing is that there is another set of types that was conceived by Toni Wolff, to whom I've referred previously. She felt that Jung's types applied more appropriately to men than they did to women. She described four types of women in terms that are more or less self-explanatory: the Amazon, the Medium, the Mother, and the Hetaira.[13] The first pair are at opposite ends of one continuum, the latter pair at opposite ends of a second continuum.

Speaking of hetairas, I'm reminded rather frivolously of a marvelous program on the potential of women, that was put on by the University of California at Berkeley a few years ago. Among the speakers was Marya Mannes, who said (and I paraphrase), "You know, I wish we could go back to Greek times and revive the notion of the hetaira. You see, if a man and a woman are living in the same house, and the man goes and sits at his desk, his position is sacrosanct, and you musn't bother him. But if a woman

13. Toni Wolff, "A Few Thoughts on the Process of Individuation in Women," *Spring 1941.* New York: Analytical Psychology Club of New York City, 1941, pp. 81–103.

sits at her desk in the home, she's up for grabs! So just think how nice it would be if one could have the pleasure of a man's company all night long, and then at eight o'clock in the morning say, 'Git!' Wouldn't that be lovely?"

Now to get back to Jung's types. His *function* types represent the four principal ways of adapting to people and things and situations. These functions operate under the aegis of the habitual *attitude;* that is, *introversion* or *extraversion*. The attitudes represent specific directions in which psychic energy, or libido, can flow. Extraversion is a flowing of energy toward the outer world, and introversion is a flowing of energy toward the inner world.

Jung believed that people are born introverted or extraverted, though at one point he did say that types might be acquired. I've had some struggles over this myself. I'm not entirely convinced that types are innate. Very small children do show marked type differences even when exposed to the same environment and subjected to the same parental influences. This I saw for myself in my own family. But the environmental influence can reinforce the basic type tendency. In England, for example, where introversion is the predominant attitude, there is universal respect toward individual privacy for which the environment provides protection in the form of strict conventions. There are all sorts of convenient *fa-çons de parler*—expressions that are not meant to be taken literally—such as, "You must come to tea one day." Americans are prone to take such pleasantries literally and immediately pull out their date books, which isn't the idea at all; it's just intended as verbal fencing with conversational gambits.

In the natural course of a person's life, extraversion and introversion may alternate as dominant attitudes. Jane and I observed this process among pre-literate peoples when we spent some time on a little pimple of an island—one of those that the British refer to as "the full stops of the Pacific"[14]—called Aitutaki. It was quite startling to us to watch the Polynesians flip back and forth from extraversion to introversion. I often had the experience of talking with a chap who one minute would be very animated and the next

14. In England, *full stop* = *period* in the U.S.

minute would stop right in the middle of a sentence and just lean up against a palm tree. He'd be off somewhere; God knows where he went! Then after about five minutes, suddenly he would plug in again and be back in business. Absolutely amazing! I've seen the Navajos do this sort of thing, too. But in our highly competitive society, one of the attitudes is more or less dammed up in order to produce a supposedly more efficient performance. As a result a definite, one-sided type is established. However, it's never possible to suppress completely the opposite attitude, as both are basic psychological factors in every individual.

People with a dominantly extraverted attitude tend to explain things in environmental terms, to regard personality characteristics as produced by outer influences. An extravert, who is unconscious of the introverted side, values the outer object and fears the inner self. In our emphatically extraverted country this attitude is evident in our love of groups, good mixers and outgoing people. An introverted English friend of mine once remarked that the only place Americans seem to consider it normal to be alone is in the bathroom. She supposed the bathroom must be to Americans what the family chapel is to the English.

Extraverts are at ease in the outer world with objects, people, and situations. Their attitude toward the object is romantic and adventurous. They are likely to look on any subjective activity as "morbidly introspective." When working with their unconscious material, they are ill at ease—as introverts are in the outer world—feeling their way with caution, reserve, and fear, as though dealing with an uncanny power. On the other hand, extraverts will jump into new situations easily without a moment's hesitation. Their contact with the object must be immediate. When they make a mistake, it hardly touches them, and they may be caught again in the same kind of error.

Left to itself, extraverted energy becomes compulsive, and this compulsive aspect can be checked only when the unconscious, introverted side is made conscious and accepted. The danger for such types is that both body and soul may be neglected because neither is obviously objective. They get into a business, and then because the business requires their attention, they expend energy beyond their innate needs and physical resources and pay the penalty with physical and psychological disorders. Or else they mismanage the business because infantilism or egotism creeps in unconsciously.

This latter fact was forcefully brought home to me during World War II. At that time there were very few psychiatrists in the Bay Area. As a matter of fact, instead of the four or five hundred psychiatrists now practicing in the region between Santa Rosa and San Jose, there were only about ten of us. All the rest in this area were in the armed forces, and we at home were feeling guilty. To make things worse, it suddenly became respectable for people to be neurotic because it got to be known that neuropsychiatric military discharges were being given at the rate of a thousand a day. So this small band of guilt-ridden analysts was trying to work twelve and fourteen hours at a stretch. It didn't do any of us any particular good, and I ended up in bed with tuberculosis for six months.

This is the kind of thing extraverts are likely to do, to drive themselves too far. I well remember meeting Esther Harding during this period. She asked me how many patients I saw in a day. "How many do *you* see?" I countered. "Five at the most," she replied, "Now, how many do you see?" I answered that I tried not to see more than twelve; she winced, saying "That's malpractice." She was right, of course.

Extraverts tend to have a constant need to make appeals for attention and to produce impressions upon their milieu. Or they have an exaggerated intimacy with those around them and a tendency to adjust to their surroundings through imitation. The more neglected the subjective, introverted side, the more primitive and infantile it becomes. When extraverts talk about themselves, they seem naive or superficial to introverts because they are so unfamiliar with their subjective sides. Their degree of well-being depends really on the extent to which they have accepted their subjective needs, for the introverted side, as I said before, is never wholly obliterated.

With the introvert, energy flows away from the object to the subject. The following quotation from Virginia Woolf's *A Room of One's Own* gives a good picture of an introvert at work:

Thought—to call it by a prouder name than it deserved—had let its line down into the stream. It swayed, minute after minute, hither and thither among the reflections and the weeds, letting the water lift it and sink it, until—you know the little tug—the sudden conglomeration of an idea at the end of one's line: and then the cautious hauling of it in, and the careful laying of it out?[15]

Of course, her whole book is a paean of praise to introversion.

Unlike the extravert, the introvert's subjective reaction to the outer stimulus is the most important thing. Introverts abstract from their environment whatever they need to satisfy their inner processes. Exposed to objective situations they become timid and anxious or else aggressive. They may be shy, taciturn, impenetrable. They insist on personal privacy, and they respect that of others. Extraverts come out to you, but introverts, while they may be feeling perfectly friendly, can make you feel excluded. They may give the impression of having ulterior motives, but actually they are holding you at arm's length so you will not become a problem to them. They are not naive; rather, they detach themselves in order to understand the other fellow before committing themselves. When introverts choose friends, it's a serious business. They usually have fewer and deeper relationships than extraverts.

Due to the fact that in modern times, in this country especially, the objective world is valued far more than the subjective, introverts may be made to feel inferior to extraverts. (Not in Zürich, though, if you move in Jungian circles!) Therefore, introverts may develop the psychology of the underdog and become egotistical and domineering. Naturally, introverts honor their introversion and thus are in better touch with their inner resources than are extraverts. This of course promotes self-knowledge and self-understanding.

Subordinate to introversion or extraversion are the four methods of adaptation, the aspects of the personality that Jung called *functions: sensation, intuition, thinking,* and *feeling.* As he has succinctly put it, a person sees something with the sensation function, classifies or puts a name to it with the thinking function,

---

15. New York: Harcourt Brace Jovanovich, © 1957, p. 5.

evaluates it with the feeling function, and estimates its possibilities with the intuitive function. Most of us have one or two developed functions, while the others are relatively undeveloped and lie more or less unavailable in the unconscious. The easiest method of determining which are the developed functions is to observe how individuals work themselves out of a jam: do they think their way out; do they wait for a hunch or an intuition; do they use observation or sensation to find loopholes; or do they try to solve the problem with feeling through another person?

The superior (developed) and inferior (undeveloped) functions are equally potent in everyone; but whereas the individual can rule the superior one, the inferior one inevitably rules the individual. For example, a thinking type can direct the thinking process but is very vulnerable on the feeling side; feelings are easily hurt and may explode volcanically. In this case feeling is the inferior function, though it may appear quite powerful to both the subject and to close associates. The feeling type, on the other hand, is vulnerable on the thinking side. When hit too hard there, the individual becomes emotional; "thinkings" have been hurt! That's what it amounts to, I assure you. Actually the superior function can often be spotted by pinpointing the inferior one. A direct hit on the inferior function will produce an emotional explosion, and that quite frequently is the tip-off.

According to Jung, people gather data with their *perceptive* functions; i.e., sensation or its opposite, intuition. These functions he calls *irrational*. The data are then processed by the *rational, assessing,* or *judging* functions, which are *thinking,* at one end of the processing spectrum and *feeling* at the other.

*Sensation.* Sensation is a perceptive function. The extraverted types are realists. They are able to retain a great many objective, unrelated facts. They're constantly receiving impressions from the concrete world, and the more extraverted they are, the less they assimilate these impressions. They are always on the hunt for new experiences, most often using each new experience only as a stepping stone to the next, regardless of their subjective needs. Extraverted sensation types could be described as sensual, inasmuch as they pursue physical enjoyments, but their conception of enjoyment might be very disagreeable to many people. They will exert themselves to astounding degrees, finding pleasure in the greatest physical hardships or the most extreme danger, for instance, Sir Edmund Hillary or Ernest Hemingway. They can also experience reality in its abstract, aesthetic aspect. They may appear to be materialists, and yet their attitude toward reality can rise to spiritual heights. Surely extraverted sensation types are the most practical of all and the best at adjusting their lives to their circumstances. If their sensation runs away with them, if they are enslaved to those things that provide sensation to the extent that they lose touch with their own inner point of view, they can become mere pleasure-seekers or perhaps scheming dissipators. When this happens, they are likely to fall prey to their neglected intuition, which can then turn negative and overwhelm them with superstitions and weird imaginings.

Now for introverted sensation, a very different thing: when differentiated, it is finely tuned and spiritual, not limited to actual physical sensation. It is perhaps the most inarticulate of the functions and finds its best expression in color or form. Jung says introverted sensation has a preferential object determination, and those objects that release the strongest sensation are decisive to the individual's psychology. An introverted sensation type described herself to me in this way: "When I am in a situation or see an object, I have an inner physical attitude; it is as though my mind were only a part of my reactive system. I sense it to the ends of my fingers. It is like going into a dark room without seeing or hearing but knowing that someone is there and knowing, too, whether the situation is favorable or unfavorable, dangerous or safe." The same woman also said to me, "I go into the outside world as long as I get subjective reactions to it. When they cease to come, I go away by myself and boil these past reactions down to abstractions. Once they are set down on paper or in paint and put away, I feel satisfied and am ready to meet the world again." The introverted sensation artist works from inner premises. A group of artists using the same model will produce totally different pictures. It is impossible to predict what will impress them and what will not because they are dominated by the inner image. This type often uses the expression, "I sense that this is such and such." The word *sense* aptly describes the process.

I should interject here that none of these types is exclusive—it's only a matter of emphasis. Obviously everyone has everything, but in varying degrees. The great majority of us are heavily loaded and heavily weighted at one or the other end of one or the other spectrums.

*Intuition.* At the opposite end of the perceptive spectrum is intuition. Intuition is an unconscious form of perception, directed in the extravert toward outer objects and in the introvert toward inner contents. It appears to be an attitude of expectation, as it is concerned with seeing possibilities in things and having hunches. It is the most useful function where there is nothing concrete to show the way; it would be an excellent attribute in a pioneer, for example. It operates when there are no facts, no moral guidelines, no proven theories, only possibilities and unknowns. Objects and facts hold no more than a transient interest for intuitives and then only as stepping stones. They tend to disregard objects to such an extent that they may be clumsy and stumble over obvious obstacles.

In conversation, intuitives leap from point to point, to the consternation of sensation types, who need to fill in all the gaps, and they hate repetition. They live either in the future or in the past, feeling most uncomfortable in the present. Consequently they react principally in anticipation or in retrospect, while drawing a blank on immediate experience. When the White Queen in *Alice in Wonderland* talks about "jam yesterday and jam tomorrow but never jam today," it seems to me, the intuitive, just like business as usual. However, to my wife, a sensation type, it seems utterly ridiculous.

Intuitives also have staring eyes that can make you feel they're looking right through you; but don't worry, they're probably not seeing a thing. I'm reminded at this point of Freud who, as I've said, was a marked sensation type. One of the comments he made about his introduction of the couch into the furniture scheme of the consulting room was that he simply didn't see how he could sit around all day with people peering at him. You know, my patients peer at me, and I don't seem to notice it too much. Of course, it just happens that the way my office is arranged I'm usually looking into full sunlight, and that might have something to do with it!

Another important thing about intuitives is that they relate very poorly to their bodies. Through neglect of their sensation side they often develop ulcers or become undernourished and register fatigue only when it is far advanced. There was a mysterious thing that used to take place with my secretary, who has a sensation function like a rock, needless to say. I would come in at two or three o'clock in the afternoon, after a teaching session or something, feeling very peaked, and she would say the most amazing thing: "Did you have any lunch?" Absolutely illuminating! Of course I hadn't had any lunch, which was why I felt so bad, but that never would have occurred to me. Intuitives tend to be physically stoical, sometimes owing merely to unawareness. They go around saying how brave they are, but the fact of the matter is that their synapses are so inefficient that they don't get the message; their dendrites are all curled up.

If these types neglect their inferior sensation, their heads are likely to soar into the clouds while their feet leave the ground. Two patients of Jung's, both of them lop-sided intuitives, come to mind in this connection. One dreamt she was up in a balloon, but not content with that, she proceeded to climb on top of it! The other had such a terrible relation to her body that Jung said to her, "You know, you act as if you've never seen your body." To which she responded blithely, "Oh, I haven't for years." So he went on, "Well, I don't like to pry, but do you know about bathing?" And she replied, "Oh, yes, yes, I always bathe under a sheet!"

Extraverted intuitives have a special ability to ferret out the potential in people, and for that reason they may do very well as therapists or educators. Their thinking tends to be of a speculative nature. On the staff of London's St. Bartholomew's Hospital, where I took my medical training, there was a man named Lord Horder who was a brilliant physician and diagnostician; he was the King's personal physician, actually. He conducted weekly rounds that were magnificent performances attended by all and sundry. One day, with a long retinue of social workers and students and residents and interns, he stopped in front of a bed and said, "Wheelwright, have a look at that chap." I went over, and there was this man lying in bed with no visible symptoms. I did what seemed to me the most sensible thing to do: I looked out the window for some time. But nothing came to me, so I had a go at the ceiling, and that did it. It all came very clear; there was no doubt in my mind. I turned around with a broad smile and announced in a tone of utmost confidence, "Lord Horder, sir, this man is suffering from pulmonary tuberculosis."

I've never seen a man turn puce so quickly. He fumed at me, "As a matter of fact, he *is* suffering from pulmonary tuberculosis, but that is absolutely irrelevant! How you ever knew it, God only knows. Do you know that there is a diagnostic method that doctors have developed? It came about because a chap once had some beer in a hogshead and he didn't know the level of the liquid, so he began to thump on the hogshead. We call it percussion. You could have tried that on this chap; you know, we do it on the chest." Then he went on, "I see something sticking out of your pocket; I believe it's called a stethoscope. You could have put that to his chest, and if you were thoughtful, you would warm it first on the palm of your hand. And you would say to him, 'My dear chap, say after me, *"ninety-nine."*' Did you do any of those things? No! Did you use your voice? You know you might have; we do that quite often. You might have said, 'What brings you here, my good man?'"

I felt very crushed and said to myself, "Well, I'm really not going to be a smash hit as a doctor." And as a matter of fact I guess I never really was. I never think of us in psychiatry as real doctors. In fact, I think the medical model is actually antithetical to analysis, as I mentioned earlier.

Apropos of this, another thing that Gray and Jane and I came up with using our tests was that, in a sample of approximately two thousand physicians, the percentage of sensation types in all the "respectable" branches of medicine was very high: eighty to eighty-five percent. It was only in psychiatry that the situation was reversed. Psychiatry is a happy hunting ground for us intuitives because we are not required to touch bodies; in fact, it is positively discouraged in the circles in which I move!

Now for introverted intuition, which is a very different kind of thing. Introverted intuitives draw on the deepest layers of the unconscious. Endowed with vision in the sense of being able to perceive things not explicitly represented, they manage to escape the pitfalls of sensation types who can get bogged down in a welter of facts and details. It is a particularly useful function for psychologists whose work is of a pioneering sort and deals with intangibles. I have mentioned previously that this is the predominant type among Jungian analysts and that Jung himself was strongly oriented in this direction. However, Jung's leading function was thinking. This would have been very difficult to determine except for the fact that what gave him the most trouble was feeling. It was one of those instances where one could pinpoint the type by recognizing the inferior function. Jung himself confirmed this in that lovely BBC film, *Face to Face,* that John Freeman made with Jung some years ago in Zürich. In it Jung states that thinking is his superior function.

There's another thing I'd like to say about introverted intuitives. I've found that the people I can work with best as an analyst and the people who have been nearest and dearest to me as peers, as patients, and as gurus, have been introverted intuitive thinking types. Apparently it is the shared intuition that makes the bridge. And besides, there's all the stimulation that comes from working with a fellow who lives at the other end of the spectrum. And, too, this is the enormously exciting thing about being married to your opposite: if you don't punch her or him in the nose, you can have the most thrilling experience in the world because of it. On the other hand, Jung was once asked, "What if two similar types married each other?" and he said, "They'd die of boredom in a month." (That was not on the record!)

*Thinking.* There are two kinds of thinking, which is an assessing function. There is the kind that derives from objective data and the kind that may be traced to a subjective source. The latter type, introverted thinking, has a subjective, inner direction and involves the development of a vague inner image or idea that has a mythological quality. It has little to do with objective fact and is acceptable to the objective world only when it is adjusted to the outer facts. The other aspect, extraverted thinking, has an outer direction and involves the intellectual reconstruction of concrete actuality or generally accepted ideas. It is the only kind approved by modern Western standards. The gauge by which thinking can be considered extraverted or introverted is this: where does it lead back to? Does it go back to established theories, external facts—as with, say, an engineer—or does it remain an abstraction and return to the subject, as with many philosophers? Jung cites Darwin as a normal extraverted thinking type and Kant as a normal introverted thinking type. Extensity is the extravert's aim, while intensity is the introvert's.

The clash between these two kinds of thinking comes about when an extraverted thinker tries to disprove the subjective abstractions of an introvert by relating them to objective facts, or when an introverted thinker takes the objective conclusions of an extravert and subordinates them to subjective ideas. This results, of course, not in greater understanding but in mutual depreciation. Actually both points of view are essential to balanced thinking. A person who has ideas and cannot explain them intelligibly becomes a total loss. Introverted abstractions save extraverted thinking from a materialistic or repetitious state, and extraverted objectivity saves introverted thinking from abstractions unrelated to the experience and traditions of society in general.

Extraverted thinking is responsible for a great mass of disconnected scientific data that is neither related to personal experience nor cemented by any subjective philosophy. Extraverted thinkers try to condition their whole lives and the lives of those around them to intellectual formulae that they construct from objective data. It is an attempt to establish absolute truth. If such people are not too rigid, they can be useful reformers, but they can also turn into disgruntled, domineering critics. These are socially-minded extraverts who have lost touch with their feelings through overvaluation of their thinking function. They may follow an ideal—often a Christian one—so blindly that they end up quite oblivious of the extent to which they are actually playing for public approval. They can even become ruthless, claiming that the end justifies the means. In our country someone who is a pillar of society and of the church may appear to the outside world as a humanitarian but to the family as a tyrant. (Many of the Puritans were like this; I speak with some feeling, having been brought up in Boston!) When such people sacrifice their lives to an impersonal ideal, they become destructive, suspicious, petty, moody, and full of hatred. This is the price that they—and their families—pay for the neglect of the inferior feeling function. Their personal side becomes overassertive to counterbalance their exaggerated, impersonal life. They will tolerate no criticism. The impersonal idea can be magnified to such a pitch that it obliterates all other ideas and becomes like a religion. But it should be remembered that all this refers to pathological one-sidedness, that normal extraverted thinking is constructive, not depreciatory. It always strives to replace worn-out or broken-down ideas with fresh new ones.

Introverted thinkers are likely to be inarticulate because they are forever trying to express the images that come to them from the unconscious and which, more often than not, fail to tally with objective facts. In trying to get their ideas across they seldom bother to present them in generally comprehensible terms, but spill them out as they are with little consideration for the requirements of their audience. They operate on the assumption that since their theses are clear to them, they will therefore be clear to others. Then if, as commonly occurs, they find themselves misunderstood, they tend to become annoyed and to depreciate the understanding and intelligence of others. This tendency can lead individuals of the type to fall under the domination of persons of a different type, especially of the opposite sex; looking upon such persons as inferior leaves the introverted thinking individual unguarded and consequently highly vulnerable to being dominated by them.

Because of their difficulty in being objective about their own creative ideas, introverted thinkers are seldom good teachers; they neglect to adapt their material to the intellectual capacity and needs of their pupils. They can also get overly involved with details and are painfully conscientious about including and considering every aspect of their theories, even taking care to bring in contrary opinions. However, this type may have the power to originate ideas or theories based on known but apparently unrelated facts. Mendeleyev, for instance, achieved this in his construction of the table of atomic weights. He left blank spaces for substances that were later discovered and found to fit in the scheme according to his predictions.

*Feeling.* Feeling is an assessing function and the feeling type has very definite likes and dislikes. As I see it, this type chooses friends on the basis of character rather than of mutual interests. The feeling function has an appraising aspect that cuts like a knife and is orderly and consistent. This is what makes it a rational, judging function even while it has a marked personal quality. One of the shadow potentials a feeling type must watch out for and be responsible about is the tendency of the feeling function to indulge in manipulation. Thinking types are particularly vulnerable to manipulation by feeling types, and the latter must be constantly on guard to make sure they aren't up to some kind of unconscious hanky-panky at an intellectual's expense.

According to Jung, feeling types are more common among women, and the results of our type test confirmed that this is indeed the case. The fact that these findings accord with the general bias that feeling is the normal function for women is one of the reasons I question whether types are actually built in at the factory. When the feeling function does occur in men, it is often a problem because such men do not conform to the stereotyped notion that all men are thinkers. I'm not entirely satisfied that societal pressures don't play a part in type determination. I wonder, for instance, how the distribution of scores on our test would look in a very introverted country that puts a high value on thinking—the China I knew in 1930–31, for example.

Being determined by social standards, extraverted feeling values are traditional and collectively valid. To quote Jung,

> "[Extraverted feeling is] under the spell of traditional or generally accepted values of some kind. I may feel moved, for instance, to say that something is 'beautiful' or 'good,' not be-

cause I find it 'beautiful' or 'good' from my own subjective feeling about it, but since it is fitting and politic to call it so, since a contrary judgment would upset the general feeling situation. A feeling judgment of this kind is not by any means a pretence or lie, it is simply an act of adjustment."[16]

Fashions owe their existence to the feeling function, as does the far more valuable, widely-based support of the whole spectrum of social, philanthropic, and similar cultural enterprises. In such areas as these, extraverted feeling demonstrates its creative aspects.

Men of the extraverted feeling type are often found functioning successfully in the ministry, in psychology, and in the arts, but in most other walks of life they are under a severe handicap. A man is commonly supposed to be a thinking creature, and it is difficult for him to maintain his masculinity against this social prejudice. He may have the ability to think, but only at such times as his thinking is supported by his feeling. That's something I've found in my personal experience. I've often struggled to bring my thinking function up from the basement and have actually made it as far as the ground floor on occasion. However, if I have a good connection with an audience or a friend, my thinking function works quite well. If I don't, disaster ensues. Writing, for instance, is pure torture because I have to do it alone. When it comes to thinking, I have no originality; a feeling-type woman, who will have a thinking animus, is better off in this regard. Such originality as I may have resides in my differentiated functions, feeling and intuition. On the other hand, it is through the inferior function that I get to my creativity.

When extraverted feeling becomes exaggerated, the unconscious, subjective, egotistical attitude slips in and renders the feeling function untrustworthy, cold, and materialistic. At its worst it causes the individual to become vicious, to put other people in a bad light while managing to appear blameless and even worthy. I knew an intellectual, thinking type woman who had a feeling type cousin. This feeling woman used to say to her friends, "Poor Maude, she simply doesn't know how to get along with people.

---

16. CW 6, par. 595.

We must do everything we can to make things easy for her." Thus she subtly depreciated Maude while at the same time putting herself in a generous and humane light. Needless to say, the results for Maude were disastrous. When Maude told me this story, she was eighty-one, and it had taken place when she was about nineteen. Yet in the midst of relating it, she burst into uncontrollable weeping; her cousin had really cut her to ribbons, which of course was exactly the cousin's unconscious intention.

Introverted feeling types are quite unlike extraverted feeling types. Their feeling arises from a vague inner image resembling that of the introverted thinking type. To get this image across, artistic talent is most helpful. Introverted feeling types frequently find it difficult to talk in analysis, and I think it may have been with them that Jung first started using paintings and drawings. This type tends to break with traditional values, as their ideas—deriving from the basic historical patterns of the mind—are very original.

Almost hostile to the object, introverted feelers can be inaccessible and silent, appearing indifferent and unfeeling, especially if the outer world presses too hard and has no connection with their inner images. Insecure in their surroundings, they may present a dull or even childlike appearance that masks their real personalities. Needing to protect themselves from the external environment, they sometimes belittle or depreciate it. They seem to have a world of their own to which they escape, and where they are at ease. Their behavior may be quite unrelated to the actual circumstances and people around them.

Introverted feeling is more intensive than extensive because it is not drained off by an easy adjustment to the outer world. When it has been too long bottled up, it will be expressed in some dramatic or exaggerated act that is inappropriate to the situation and consequently not appreciated. Individuals of this type often express themselves secretly or allow their emotional intensity to flow unnoticed into those dependent upon them. In an attempt to hold their own against their outer environment, they may try to dominate it. This domination is not disturbing unless it is egotistical; then it becomes a kind of ambition or trickery, especially with women of this type.

There are a few miscellaneous comments that I'd like to end with. For one thing, the evaluating role of feeling has been made much of, but there has been little talk about the relating aspects of feeling. Relating is usually, in Jungian circles, thought to be a monopoly of the anima in men, just as thinking is often considered a monopoly of the animus. So I would like to see some strong, vigorous person, who has a lot more energy than I have at this point, do a piece of research on where feeling leaves off and the anima begins. James Hillman[17] has made some helpful comments on this subject.

I know many thinking-type men who do not have a developed feeling function but who, nevertheless, manifest great kindness and sensitivity. I would cite my friend Erik Erikson as an example of such a man. He was terribly good at working with children, toward whom he exhibited a kind of tenderness and a nurturant quality that were extraordinary. However, he is very sophisticated about Jungian matters; he knows about the anima, and he lets her function, no doubt about it. On the other hand, while relating has been the most important thing to me throughout my whole life, I think that my relating is done not with my anima but with my feeling function. My anima does do a rather good job for me sometimes in playing messenger, the way she's supposed to, between my unconscious and my conscious, but she also has a rather annoying way of appearing negatively, making me appear moody or pettish. In any case, I would really like to see more work done on the relating aspect of the feeling function.

For another thing, it has been clinically observed that there is a marked type linkage with the animus and the anima. Hence this business of polar-opposites marrying each other. One usually falls in love with somebody who is, type-wise, one's polar opposite. I think that's something else that could bear study.

Again, I commented about feeling types having to be very much on the look-out for their manipulations, but something else for them to watch out for is identifying with the superior function.

17.See James Hillman, "The Feeling Function," in Marie-Louise von Franz and James Hillman, *Lectures on Jung's Typology.* New York: Spring Publications, 1971, *and* James Hillman, "Anima," *Spring 1973.* New York: Spring Publications, 1973, pp. 97–132.

This can be a problem for any of the types, of course, and is awfully easy to do, especially when the function is working well. What happens is that the I, the ego, tends to become synonymous with the superior function, when in fact the superior function should be in the service of the ego.

I also want to mention two more points about types and their shadow aspects. One is that Jungians are likely when hard pressed to use their type as an alibi. You'll find somebody like me saying, "Ah, well, you can't really expect me to be able to think, you know, old chap; I'm a feeling type." It's an easy way out, so one has to watch for that.

Another point is something that occurs as a result of cultural prejudice. Among Jungians, with their tremendously high incidence of intuitives, sensation types tend to be undervalued, because they are terribly awkward for us intuitives. They're like burrs under a saddle, always producing those annoying things called facts that just spoil any nice, free-floating discussion one might be having. But if it were not for the sensation types, I think the Jung Institute here in San Francisco would have been in the hands of the receivers some years ago. They can do all kinds of esoteric things: they know about chi-square; they can add figures; it's amazing! Without them we'd be absolutely lost; but at the same time the intuitive majority complains about them. It's very interesting how few of them there are in the Jungian world. Christine Mann, who worked together with Esther Harding and Eleanor Bertine for a long while, was one. My wife is one. Violet de Laszlo is another. Mrs. Jung was, and Mary Briner in Zürich is. Toni Frey, who runs the clinic on the Zürichberg, is, and so is John Buehler, who invented the scoring for our test. And I was delighted to find that several of the new crop of candidates at the Institute are sensation types.

For some strange reason the subject of types seems until recently to have been very neglected in Jungian training centers. Perhaps this had something to do with the fact that Jung moved on in his later years to a passionate exploration of the collective unconscious. In so doing, he left types behind, except incidentally, and most of his followers moved with him. Being atypical, I have never been able to forget them even for a day. And now, in my old age, I am focused on the morphology, classification and interrelations of seashells. This new passion demands endless introverted sensation and thinking. So, at long last, the sleeping giant is stirring.

# *Marriage in the Second Half of Life*[18]

This is a subject that holds rather more than an academic interest for me. I am not talking about giving up and getting married again, after the bell has rung at midnight of one's 35th year. I am talking about working it through with the same husband or wife that you started off with. Centrally important to my thesis are the notions of the animus and the anima and of psychological types. In connection with the man-woman relationship, I think it is interesting to mention that in psychoanalytic circles, at least until very recently, few people argued against Freud's dictum that a woman is an inferior creature

---

18. An altered version of this chapter was first published as "Reflections on Marriage in the Second Half of Life," *Quadrant,* vol. 8–9, Fall/Winter, 1970–71, pp. 26–31.

who wishes she had a penis. This derogation of women has not prevailed among Jungians. I am fond of saying to my Freudian friends that the penis doesn't enjoy quite the prestige in Jungian circles that it does in Freudian circles. It is also of interest that my friend Erik Erikson, whose voice carries a great deal of weight, was the first psychoanalyst to write that it was high time to stop describing women in terms of what they had not got. He then developed his notion about what he calls *productive enclosed inner spaces*.

Now, I suppose that to talk about marriage in the second half of life one really has to say at least something about how it all begins. Plato's *Symposium* contains a fanciful description of circular original beings who were split in half by an angry Zeus and, thereafter, ". . . each desiring his other half, came together, and throwing their arms about one another, entwined in mutual embraces, longing to grow into one . . ."[19] This image always comes to mind when I see young people falling in love, and when I see the kind of fusion that occurs and the massive projections of animus and anima. Of course, psychological types are very much linked with animus and anima in this process. It is a very difficult and complicated business, but I think that any of us working clinically with marriage problems will see that very often they first present themselves in terms of clashes around type differences. The husband, let us say, is very sloppy around the house, which may get the wife terribly upset. She may say, "For God's sweet sake, can't you ever pick up anything after yourself? I came home today and stepped on a roller skate, etc." There are all sorts of recriminations that may occur on this basis.

I think that in the early years of marriage, sex, the great healer, very often fends off what might be a catastrophic kind of explosion. Later on—well, I am not going to say that when you get to be old, sex is no longer of any interest, but things are different from the early years. There isn't any question at all that sex has

---

19. Plato, "Symposium," in *The Dialogues of Plato*, vol. 1, translated into English by B. Jowett, M.A. New York: Random House, 1892, p. 317.

saved a lot of really head-on explosions between people who were simply not prepared or not able to go in depth into what was happening between them. I am reminded of something Erna Rosenbaum, an old friend and Jungian analyst, now dead, used to say: "Women come to sex for creation, and men come to sex for consolation."

Anyhow, pretty soon along come children, and my impression as I work with people in their middle years is that during this time a kind of symbiosis tends to get set up, and very often an equilibrium gets established on the type basis. So that when, for instance, the gruesome alarm clock goes off, and the children have to be got off to school, everyone begins to move around like a well-drilled football team and do what each does best. Zigging and zagging through the kitchen, miraculously not spilling too much oatmeal on each other, the children are finally dressed and got off to school. This takes a lot of teamwork. But the important fact is that the whole relationship tends to be in terms of the children; so that what was starting to be worked out between the parents may just have to sit around and wait—not entirely, but to a large extent. In order to be able through these years to do the best one can—not only in one's marriage, but in general—one tends to live on one's superior functions. During the middle years anything that impairs performance, including inferior functions, is likely to get suppressed. Of course this applies as well in the marriage and its whole symbiotic situation.

Finally, twenty-five years later perhaps, the time comes when Mama and Papa stand at the door and wave goodbye to little Willie, who is not little Willie anymore. By now he is twenty-one and is trudging down the path with his bundle over his shoulder to make his fortune, the last of the children to go. Mama may be crying, and Papa may be heaving a sigh of relief, but at any rate it is done. Next morning they start squirting grapefruit in each other's eyes, alone for the first time in twenty-five years. No buffer state of Manchuria anymore. No scnse talking about the children; they went. And then you are back at Position One again. But now you've reached the age where, if things really begin to get difficult and even violent, you can no longer be quite sure that sex, the great healer, will take care of it. The relationship now actually has to be worked through.

My thesis is really very simple: if a marriage is to survive in the second half of life, one has to start peeling off the projections one way or another. And usually one of the ways this happens is that after the two are back again facing each other alone, the strain becomes too great. Of course the strain may have been great for some time before. When one is in love, one so desperately wants to be what one is supposed by one's partner to be; one tries very hard to be that. But the strain gets to be hell. So somewhere along the line, something gives and the wife may say, "You know, Albert, I've put up with it all these years, but that sampler your Aunt Minnie did in cross-stitch that says 'God Bless Our Home'—it stinks; it is absolutely dreadful. I can no longer bear it!" And he goes white and reels back, and then he moves forward a little bit and says, "Well, while we are having some truths around here, let me tell you a thing or two," and then it begins to fly back and forth. He says, "I am just sick and tired of doing all the thinking around here. I am sick of trying to fix up your checkbook, and I am sick of getting things organized and trying to keep things straightened out." And she says, "Are you really! Well, I am sick of doing all the feeling around here, not only for myself but for you too. Who's always had to cope with the children? Who decided where the children should go to school? And another thing, we'd never have had anybody in this house if it hadn't been for me; it's damned lucky that any friends ever came back. I'd get somebody to come here and before long you'd generate an explosion by saying, 'let's talk about Communism. Let's talk about Catholicism.' I'd try to change the conversation to planting petunias or something bland, but no, you had to kick back on it. Why, it's a wonder we have any friends left!" So things begin to emerge in this fashion; I am sure we can all write our own versions.

Then there is another aspect one is faced with: the aging process and one's relation to it is a very central part of the whole business of marriage in the second half of life. In particular, one's attitude toward death becomes increasingly important. Americans talk about something that happens in old age; they call it disengagement. What this really means is that you are losing your grip and your connection with life. So when I start developing this theme about the business of the withdrawal of projections (which is, of course, particularly meaningful and particularly relevant to the marriage situation), people always begin to look very sad and shake their heads and talk about disengagement. Far from being disengagement, it seems to me that one's relation to people and to one's surroundings will be better to the extent that one has withdrawn one's projections. The more one can peel the projections off one's partner, the more one can love the person he or she really is. The more one defines one's ego boundaries, the more separateness there is and the more real loving can occur.

I always feel that when one is *in* love and hearing Beethoven's *Ninth* all day and all night, one is really having an ecstatic connection with an aspect of oneself; it is the anima (or animus) that does it. There's nothing quite like it, but you have to forego this ecstasy eventually. Of course, the Great American Way is that when the divine ecstasy is not there any more, you divorce and remarry. I have a sort of notion that there must be for every one of us maybe half-a-dozen people in a life span with whom we might fall in love and marry. Suppose we marry the first one of these people we meet. The chances are that we will meet at least three or four of the remaining five, and then what? Does one then divorce and remarry? This brings in the whole very complicated matter of whether one lives out a relationship outside of marriage. If you have an animus-anima thing going, and you get married, it changes into something else. I am not saying it may not be very good, but with marriage there are children, and it is in the public domain. The other thing is not; it is only between the man and the woman involved. There almost always is the shadow in it too, and, dangerous as it may sound, from my experience this seems somehow to be a necessary concomitant for the anima and animus to get assimilated.

I would like to say just a bit more about my attitude toward aging. This may be a very euphoric notion—I suspect some of my tough-minded colleagues think it is a reaction formation—but it seems to me that at approximately midnight of my thirty-fifth year my body crossed the Great Divide and started going downhill. At any rate, I notice now that it has descended quite a long way. However, as I've said elsewhere, there is energy released in the process, and that energy, I have found, begins to flow into psychic activity; there is a great increase in self-intimacy. So I have this idea that as the body goes down, the psyche climbs up. It benefits by the body "rundown," if you like; there's that much more libido available for psychic activity.

I've also noticed that there are a number of people who in one way or another are helped to make this transition. My colleague Joseph Henderson calls it *a preliminary experience of aging.* Some people, and I was lucky enough to be one of them, do have this sort of experience. During and after World War II, I got a kind of compulsive momentum going and kept right on working fourteen-hour days even after the war ended. It was insane to do that, but I had lots of rationalizations. Nevertheless, Mother West Wind was observing this phenomenon; she peered at me and thought, "Look at this bird. He's case-hardened, and how are we going to lay him low?" Then she peered again and saw that the apices of both my lungs were stuffed full of little red bugs, little TB bacilli that were lying dormant. So she threw a thunderbolt or something like that at me, it exploded, and I had TB. I fought it like hell for about six weeks and then, for the next four months, went along with it. I was thrown perforce into a very long, deep, introverted process, and this helped me begin to move into the second half of life.

Thus the whole process began for me, and my wife Jane had been doing the same sort of thing in her own way. It seems to me that unless both people in a marriage are doing it, it doesn't work, at least not in terms of the marriage relationship. One begins to be busier and busier with it. I don't speculate much on what is going to happen to me when I'm dead; I don't know much about that. What I am focused on is leaving. I have seen many people die, and many have died screaming; I don't want that. In one of his seminars, Jung made a very felicitous statement to the effect that if one has discharged one's debt to one's genes and to society, one has lived oneself out of life. I thought that was beautiful. To achieve this, there is the necessity of coming to terms not only with one's past but with history and evolution and the whole archetypal level that increasingly one has to explore, one *wants* to explore, really. In addition, the withdrawal of projections has to continue.

There is something else that many psychiatrists are hung up on: the question of relinquishing ego control. At a symposium on death in which I participated at the Group for the Advancement of Psychiatry (a research group I belonged to), everyone made stirring speeches about this control stuff. It seemed very strange to me, but that is the way they talked. So I got up and said, "I can't see how a bunch of analysts who work with patients and who live with the unconscious could possibly have such megalomaniacal ideas about control. Did you never hear of Fate?" Of course, I am painfully aware that neither am I entirely immune to this matter of ego control. It is not always easy, but coming to terms with it is part of the task of aging. Now for a couple of vignettes to provide some clinical substance.

A man and woman came to us because of a marriage crisis. Jane worked with the husband, and I worked with the wife. They were about our age, which at that time would have been the mid-fifties. What had precipitated the crisis was that he had been having an affair, and she had found out about it. It was one of those situations where letters had been left around, as though he wanted it to be known, hoping to get the thing blown up. Here one gets into something very difficult, I think, and that is the question of whether or not one runs to the partner and tells what is going on. Certainly if one does it in order to be shriven, because one can't carry one's own guilt, then it is indeed a questionable thing to do. This is such a tricky thing, it seems to me, and there is no definite answer to it; at least I certainly don't know of one. In any case, he did leave a letter around, and the whole thing did blow up. Their predicament brought to mind "Marriage as a Psychological Relationship," the first piece of Jung's I ever read—in my opinion one of the best things he ever wrote—that was published in Hermann

Keyserling's *The Book of Marriage*[20] and has to do with the idea of the contained and the container. In this couple's marriage it appeared as though the wife were the container, and the husband were the contained, that she mothered him; at one level this actually was the case. But something very interesting developed in the relationship that I have seen happen not infrequently. Although at a certain level one of the partners may be the container, at a deeper level it turns out that the other one is the container. They are both busy being containers at different levels. And indeed, this is what had developed with them.

As the analysis proceeded, two things happened to the husband. The first came out of the fact that Jane did not play the mother for him in the analytic relationship. To invoke Franz Alexander's concept of corrective emotional experience, when the analyst doesn't turn out to be the devil that your father or mother was, you begin to have direct, firsthand experience of parental relationships and to be able gradually to see through your projections and get that aspect of the animus and anima integrated into your conscious psyche. I'm guessing, but I think this was one of the things that may have occurred with him, so that as a result his containedness quit. The other thing that happened was that he experienced the backside of his ego—his shadow, that is—at the gut level. These were the most important things for his side of the relationship and freed him up, but the change in him threw his wife into a sudden panic. She had the following dream:

> *I was on the bed of a truck, and it had a cab, as pickup trucks do. My husband was driving, and as we went along I saw a tiger walking along through the grass. The tiger began to move faster, and I saw it was beginning to gain on the truck. I banged on the window of the cab, trying to get my husband's attention so that he would take me in with him or do something. He paid no attention and just kept driving along very slowly. The tiger came closer and closer and finally gave a great spring (it was a female tiger), and the dream ended.*

---

20. New York: Harcourt Brace, 1926; later translated by H. G. and Cary F. Baynes and published in *Contributions to Analytical Psychology*. New York: Harcourt Brace, 1928; and later translated by R. F. C. Hull and published in CW 17.

This dream uncovered *her* containedness in *him*. Her relationship to her mother had been very poor, and she had been completely contained in her father. So of course she had projected the father-thing onto her husband, and now that blew up. This helped to peel off an awful lot of projected animus-anima stuff, and while all that peeling was going on, there was also some type-peeling getting accomplished. She was a feeling type with inferior thinking, and he the opposite. She began to resign from doing his feeling for him, saying, "I am terribly sorry, but I am just going to hand in my ticket; you'll have to do it yourself, Kid." And he said, "Very well, and why don't you do a little thinking, Honey, if you don't mind." She did mind, but at any rate, both of them began trying. So I'll end that one there.

It seems to me that if one is truly going to make it in marriage, one has to be immensely hooked on the growth process. I look upon this not as any great virtue nor any great "unvirtue." It seems to me that some of us are just stuck with it. I get terribly resentful sometimes when I'm driving along and see a farmer working his fields. I think, "Goddamn, wouldn't that be nice! All there is for him is the wind and the rain and the sun, and here I have to go back and have more analysis, and I am 70 years old; to hell with it!" And yet I just can't help it, you know, it is just too damn bad about me. And it's too damn bad about all of us Jungians. Really, we are just stuck with it. I expect introverts would phrase it more positively, but I think one has to be stuck with it, because this also has to do with "living oneself out of life." Dying is surely part of the growth process. I can't think of an event that is more important, except perhaps getting born, and it takes a lot of homework. For my own part, there has been no day since I was fifty that I haven't thought of death and specifically of my own. I need to do this.

I guess I would like to end this discussion by speaking of a character in a play of T. S. Eliot's with whom I am sure most of you are familiar. I'm referring to Celia Coplestone and to *The Cocktail Party*. You will remember that she has a very stylized interview with a very stylized psychiatrist named Sir Harcourt Riley, in the course of which she tells him that she is suffering from a terrible sense of sin. Then she says something that endeared her to me very much, because I have always thought there is a difference between legitimate and illegitimate guilt. It seems to me that one of the marks of maturity lies in the degree to which one can carry one's legitimate guilt. One surely has done things that are according to one's own value system just plain bad, and the question is can one carry it or not? Or must one have somebody to shrive one? One needs to be pretty grown-up to carry this kind of stuff around.

Celia makes this point, and she says in effect: you know I am suffering from this awful sense of guilt. It is not the fact that for the last six months I have been the mistress of my best friend's husband. It's not that. Those things happen. But what is so awful is that there is more in me than I am developing. There is more in me than I am being. I am cheating on my own potential. That's the sin.

# *Finis*[21]

One's experience of the aging process tends to be colored or even determined by the culture context in which one lives. In other words, the collective attitudes and prejudices toward aging that have hammered upon a person all through his younger years gradually become incorporated into his own value system and adopted as his own subjective attitude. The culture context varies widely in different parts of the world. In China, for example, one looks forward to old age with great eagerness, for it is the halcyon time in one's life span. Old age is not only respected but actually revered. The old one is the carrier of wisdom; he stands in the gateway that leads to history and tradi-

---

21. Boundary, border, limit, end, purpose, aim, extreme limit, summit, highest degree, starting point, goal, death.

tion, so he can be concerned with historical and impersonal trends rather than with small day-to-day events.

The following two incidents, that occurred when I was living in Peking around 1930, will perhaps help throw light on the Chinese attitude. The first occurred when a friend of mine and I were studying Chinese. Our tutor, as was characteristic of the teaching method at that time, spoke no English. After a few weeks we began to realize that Chinese verbs did not have past and future tenses. We then realized that there must be a prefix that one attached to a verb to indicate past or future. Since we were becoming somewhat bored with confining our conversation to the present, we conveyed to our tutor the wish to learn these prefixes. He soon caught on, pointed over his shoulder, and said with a smile, *"Hou-lai,"* then pointed in front of him and said, *"Ts'ung-t'ien."* We were pleased and thought, "Aha! *Ts'ung-t'ien* means *in the future* and *hou-lai* means *in the past."* There were some moments of utter confusion a little later when we learned that the meanings of the words were exactly the reverse; our tutor's gestures indicated that the natural Chinese orientation was to face the past and back steadfastly into the future.

A related value was dramatically displayed by the same tutor some months later. He arrived one morning at my house with his old father and his young son. They all put their hands together and shook them and bowed. And then my tutor, standing in the middle, made a sweeping motion with his hand. Starting with his father, he said, *"Fu-ch'in, Wo, Ti-ti,"* meaning, "Father, I, little brother." They then bowed again and filed out with the old one leading the procession, naturally. I finally figured out that this was meant to convey that the individual was relatively unimportant, that it was the historical continuum that really mattered.

Europe represents a kind of halfway house in its attitude toward old age. Since the European ethos is predominantly introverted, Europeans value the inner world very highly, although not so exaggeratedly as was the case in China. However, they generally observe the important principle—although I have never heard this formulated by a European—that the time to start preparing for old age is while one is still young. Salvatore Lucia, of the University of California, has postulated that old age begins at birth, and this seems to me a fair enough statement. In any case, one finds in England and on the Continent that men and women begin very early to develop avocations that have real meaning for them. In this way they manage to circumvent one of the all-too-common American tragedies: that old age suddenly descends upon a man or woman like a thief in the night. An English friend of mine, shortly after her arrival in this country, commented that the older people she saw did not look as if they had aged, but rather as if they had sustained a severe shock.

The American attitude toward old age is at the opposite end of the spectrum from the Chinese. The collective attitude in America worships youth and derogates old age. As one might expect, this point of view is accompanied by a tremendous over-valuation of extraversion and object orientation. While in recent times the increase in life expectancy has occasioned much concern with the problem of old age, the collective prejudice has persisted, and Americans continue to approach old age as though it were a combination of an economic liability and an illness. It is still a commonplace to hear medical men referring in disparaging terms to those old crocks who clutter up their waiting rooms.

In the face of such an attitude, old age is hardly an attractive prospect. It seems plain, then, that physicians have a responsibility to inculcate a different attitude in their patients and in their students, particularly the younger students who are not yet too set in their convictions or too threatened by finding themselves *in medias res*. One of the chief educative difficulties is in finding enough teachers who can say with Browning:

> Grow old along with me!
> The best is yet to be,
> The last of life, for which the first was made:
> . . .[22]

Unless an individual has an understanding of the aging process and an affirmative attitude toward it, it is virtually impossible to convey in a convincing way that old age is indeed a desirable

---

22. Robert Browning, "Rabbi Ben Ezra."

goal. I am bound to say, however, that in the psychological world, aging and death have recently been displacing sex as a focus of interest.

Too commonly one hears of hobbies being introduced as an ameliorative measure. In my opinion, taking up a hobby, as this is usually understood, is equivalent to taking dope to distract oneself from a painful process. But I would distinguish such hobbies from the meaningful avocations that I cited earlier as characteristic of many Europeans.

In my private practice I have found aging patients to be far more flexible than young ones. This somewhat contentious statement becomes simpler to understand when one considers the different functions of what Jung describes as the first and second halves of life. During the first half of life, people are faced with the tasks of ego mastery, of defining their ego boundaries, of fulfilling themselves in the outer world in terms of sex, marriage, children, professional achievement, standing in the community. These object-oriented tasks demand a tremendous amount of concentrated effort and inevitably require the mobilization of one's best psychological equipment. This is almost bound to produce a certain lopsidedness in the service of efficiency. To open Pandora's box by experimenting with relatively undeveloped potential skills might threaten a person's outer effectiveness.

By contrast, someone who has reached the age of forty or forty-five has, in all probability, achieved the maximum as far as status is concerned. (Perhaps because I was a slow starter, my peak came around sixty.) Consequently competitiveness and possessiveness become less important, and the tendency is to become more subjectively oriented. If one has gone along with the aging process, there now is nobody to compete with except oneself, and one thus grows increasingly concerned with what one is, rather than what one does. It could be said that the goal becomes a state of being that *may* result in action or, more specifically, a state of self-realization or wholeness. This necessitates a coming to terms with one's failures as well as successes and a coming to terms with history. I am struck very much by the need of older people to transcend the personal frame, but this is a point of view less well supported by the culture in this country than in Europe and considerably less so than in China, as I suggested earlier.

To sum up these two periods of life, in youth the body orientation ties one to outer physical events for life's rewards and toward middle age one becomes increasingly oriented to inner psychological events. This implies the important task of disidentifying from outer things. I would in fact define maturity as the degree to which a person has withdrawn his projections upon persons, places, and things. It appears to me fortunate that as catabolism of the body increases, there appears to be a release of energy producing the effect of increasing anabolism psychologically. More simply put, the less energy is demanded by the body, the more energy is available for psychic growth.

At this point I should like to summarize the case of a woman in her late fifties. She came to me shortly after a hospitalization that followed the completion of a big industrial consultant job. She had virtually collapsed but had no idea why she should find herself in such a plight.

Professionally she had been very successful, but disregard of her psychological problems had, as is so often the case, caused them to lodge in her body. She had a fairly long history of conversion symptoms and used what I have come to recognize as the standard conversion symptom argument: "If only I didn't have these aches and pains, I could go ahead and work and be active." She failed to see that her symptoms were devised by the unconscious precisely to prevent her from working and to force her to face her problems. It was a long time before she tumbled to this, but one day she said, "I've made a discovery. I don't need my symptoms anymore." And, from then on, there was no more conversion trouble.

As she came to grips with her psychological problems directly, she gradually began to find well-being and inner harmony more important than material achievement and to value herself for her qualities as a person rather than only in terms of output. This was contrary to the precept with which she had been raised, which was "By their deeds ye shall know them." Very attached to a gifted father, she had wanted to emulate him and consequently identified with him. She had been on bad terms with her mother who seemed to her only a *Hausfrau* living in the shadow of the father. While she did well academically, she put a low premium on femininity and regarded a woman's life as unenticing. She denied the validity of feeling, the importance of personal things, and the value of interpersonal relationships for their own sake. She was so successful throughout her youth that she did not realize she had any problem as a woman.

As she worked through her childhood relation to her mother, she began to see that it was the mother's situation and not womanhood *per se* that had made an uninteresting drudge. As her sympathies became mobilized, she began to see the positive aspects of her mother and to accept herself as a woman. One day she said, "I've been in a conventional reverse-Oedipal situation, hating my mother and loving my father, trying to win him by being like him. I've lived like a man." In fact, people constantly said of her that she "thought like a man," and it was interesting to note that her sexuality had been split off from her feeling, as a man's tends to be. In her thirties she had married an engineer much older than herself. On the surface they appeared to be quite independent of each other, but underneath she was only half a person; the other half was projected onto him. It was as though being his wife was her justification for existence.

During analysis she gradually came to realize that she had married him as a father-surrogate, but her realization of this enhanced her relationship with him rather than hurting it. As she gained separateness and wholeness, she got over one of her basic problems: her fear of her husband's death, for now she felt like a person in her own right who would not be lost without him.

The termination of her analysis was, in my opinion, ideal. One day she came in and said, "I suppose you've known for some time now that my job with you is finished. I only realized it this morning. I woke up saying to myself, 'My analysis is finished. I don't need to go to Jo Wheelwright any more.' "

She had made real headway in one of the principal tasks of analysis, the reconciling of opposites, that is to say, thesis, antithesis, resolved in synthesis. The important reconciliation was between eros and logos, which had throughout her life appeared to be mutually exclusive. Parenthetically, I would define eros as the principle of relatedness, an appreciation of interpersonal relationships for their own rewards, a respect for the dignity of other people, and a joy in giving for its own sake. Logos I would define as the capacity to view the world and situations in an impersonal way, emphasizing content and intellectual understanding. Logos says, "I am running a research project or a business and everybody who joins me is hereby forewarned that this is the most important thing. If anybody gets his feelings hurt, he can drop out."

Another important phenomenon I should like to discuss is that of preliminary experiences of the aging process. They are usually of a temporary nature and may occur fairly early in life, before the person has completed the tasks of the first half of life, regardless of his outward attitude or of the attitude of the society toward aging. These experiences of the aging process consist of, to quote my friend and colleague Joseph Henderson, "periodic episodes of relative disinterest in the outer world, with attention at these times directed toward an interest in strengthening self-identity and developing self-realization." Such episodes involve a shift of the center of gravity from the ego, the center of consciousness, to the self, the center of the total personality, both conscious and unconscious.

It is experiences of this kind that bring many men and women around forty or forty-five years of age into my office with no more specific complaint than that they are restless, discontented, bored, that their lives, though successful in the eyes of the world, have become sterile. The menopause is frequently a precipitating factor in women.

In younger people these episodes are usually generated by some disaster, such as severe financial reverses or physical or psychological illness. Tuberculosis has always interested me in this connection. (Of course, my interest could have no connection with the fact that I happen to have had a couple of bouts with the little red bugs myself!) Treatment for the illness includes a forced period of introversion, and this in turn brings about—once the limitations of the situation have been accepted—one of these intervals of relative disinterest in the outer world. (The introduction of

Isoniazid may very well remove the entire *raison d'être* for having tuberculosis at all, inasmuch as bed rest has been, for mild cases at any rate, practically eliminated.)

I think that the withdrawal from public life of Charles Lindbergh after the catastrophe of the kidnapping of his son, when he was at the peak of his fame in his chosen occupation, could be described as one of these episodes. The fact that he reemerged into the limelight in a quite different role is also characteristic of these experiences; for more often than not the return is from a different inner direction or with a radical change of attitude. This process is similar to the law of withdrawal and return formulated by Arnold Toynbee, and it also recalls the French aphorism, *il faut reculer pour mieux sauter*—one must draw back in order to make a better leap forward. And, nearer to home and at an earlier transition, there is Erikson's psycho-social moratorium of adolescence.

Another example of such a withdrawal and return is illustrated in the case of a man I know who had some years ago achieved great distinction through an invention of his in the field of optics. At the height of his career he found his marriage breaking up, and he also found himself, due to internal politics, being maneuvered out of his position in the scientific project he had helped to develop. His withdrawal consisted of a four-year hitch in the navy, at the conclusion of which he became an agriculturist. While presently no longer concerned with his public reputation, he is nevertheless functioning very fully, and the farm he operates serves as a pilot plant for a government agency concerned with agricultural research.

In any discussion of aging there is, unfortunately, no blinking the fact that at the end of the road lies death. However, if one has at least approximately fulfilled one's potential, death can then be as natural a part of life as birth. At least so it seems to me. And in the meantime I have developed a rather ghoulish way of pressing people to finding a more affirmative attitude toward the aging process. This is done simply by pointing a bony and aging finger at them and saying in an intense whisper, "You, too will be old."

# Jung
# and Wheelwright:
# Three Encounters

From the beginning I was tremendously struck by Jung's relativistic position with regard to *the truth*. During maybe the second or third appointment I had with him he asked, "Do you think you are in the right place?" Feeling enormously inferior, as I did in those days, I began to heave myself to my feet. I thought that he thought, "Well, here's this pimply-faced young man who is obviously not destined to arrive anywhere, and he isn't anybody, and I don't know why I ever agreed to give him an hour." I assumed he was getting bored and was telling me to get out. But he said, "Sit down, sit down! I didn't mean for you to get out. What I do mean to say is this: you know there are three of us—Dr. Freud, Dr. Adler and myself—who are really going great guns now in Europe (this is my lingo;

he talked in a very dignified way), and obviously no one of us has the whole truth. If any one of us did, the other two would simply be out of business in no time flat.

"Now, what it says in the storybooks on page one or two, that you must not generalize on your own psychology, is just precisely what everybody does. Freud and Adler and I are not exceptions to this rule, so our concepts are really personal confessions. We have generalized them, we have abstracted them, and we produce lots of documentation so it will appear that we based these notions upon an overwhelming body of evidence we had amassed through years of clinical practice. Don't let that fool you for a minute. The fact is that they are personal confessions. What surprises me is not so much that none of us has the whole truth, but that there are so many people who find our value systems and our attitudes and our truths congenial to them. That is what is really surprising to me.

"What I meant by that question was which one of us is right for you? Are you one of the people who should be with Freud, are you one of the people who should be with Adler, or are you one of the people who should be with me? That's all. I have a little book there that compares the three of us. Why don't you have a look at it?" I did, and I decided that I really was in the right place. Time has abundantly confirmed this.

In later years he said many times that he couldn't claim to have *the* truth, that the most he could say was that he was struggling to get to *his* truth, and that the views he expressed were just that and no more. If they were applicable and meaningful to other people, that was fine. I like this position of his very, very much.

\*    \*    \*

There was a mischievous episode with Jung that took place in 1935 or 1936 during the time I was doing my medical training in London. It was one of the few times I was ever able to put anything over on him. A woman friend of ours fell into a psychosis; she fell into schizophrenia. This friend was young, had three or four small children, and it seemed a terrible tragedy to us. We were very keen on helping her, and we thought that Jung was the only one who understood this problem, this eruption of the collective unconscious. You see, most of us Jungians have the notion that when somebody falls into a psychosis, what they have done is to tumble into the collective unconscious, which I have always equated with Freud's Id. (In my opinion Jung spent forty years really exploring the Id instead of just settling for the fact that it contained a sex drive and a power drive. This investigation of the collective unconscious actually comprised the bulk of Jung's later work.) At any rate, we felt he was the only one who could reach this woman and lead her back into life.

So I went over to Zürich and got an appointment with Jung. I began telling him about this woman, and I presented it in *feeling* terms. It was very genuine, not hammed up, but he was enormously bored. I was getting absolutely nowhere at all with him. He smoked a pipe continuously, and when he was bored had a habit of pulling the aluminum bit out of the pipe and pouring dirty spit—dirty pipe water—into a little pot on his desk. So there he was, pouring all this spit into this little pot, obviously very, very bored. Finally after about a half-hour of this, he interrupted me and said, "Look, I think I could probably see this woman; I could give her half an hour maybe in a month's time." I felt absolutely sunk. That wasn't going to do any good. This woman needed to be seen immediately, and of course, she needed all the time that it would take.

Then I thought, well, by God, you know Jung is a *thinking* type. So I took a deep breath and began to present her quite unemotionally as a very interesting problem: a woman who had been brought up in primitive surroundings and after a childhood spent in close contact with nature, had been sent across country to a sophisticated Eastern girls' boarding school and then to a very sophisticated women's college. Finally she had been thrown into a very highbrow and sophisticated social milieu. I told Jung that these two aspects of this woman's life had never been reconciled and that following the birth of her last child, she had fallen into a post-partum psychosis. What had really happened was that this split had been opened up in her—these two unreconciled things— so that in a sense what she needed to do was to reconcile the most primitive with the most civilized and sophisticated. That was the problem. By this time Jung was leaning forward at his desk, no more dirty water coming out of the pipe. He interrupted me and said, "Come on, let's go down and talk to my secretary; I'll see her tomorrow morning at seven o'clock."

Of course, I was simply overjoyed. Then I went back to London and didn't see Jung again for some time. He took our friend on, and he did reach her and lead her back into life. She has never had another schizophrenic episode. Not only did he bring her back into life, but as should happen when someone goes through a psychosis, she came out of it more by a great deal than when she went into it. In other words, she was enormously enlarged as a human being. Her consciousness was vastly expanded as a result of this tremendous experience, thanks to Jung. As he used to say, if you look at somebody floundering around in the collective unconscious with your left eye, they are crazy as hell, but if you look with your right eye, they are having the most exciting and meaningful experience any human being can have. It is true, and she came back.

Meanwhile, I returned to Zürich about six months later and attended one of Jung's seminars. After the seminar he beckoned to me and said, "You think you're pretty smart, don't you?" I really didn't remember this mischievous trick I had pulled, and I said, "What do you mean?" He said, "You know what I mean: about that woman. Actually it has been very important, but it was the way you did it." I said, "Oh, you mean all that thinking-feeling stuff. Well, you invented those things." He said, "Yes, sometimes I wish to God I never had." He was bawling me out, but he was also very amused. It made me realize that as developed as he was in many areas, there was no question but that feeling was his inferior function.

\*   \*   \*

I like to tell this next story because it is so characteristic of Jung. Just before war broke in Europe, I had my last hour with Jung; it must have been in July or August of 1938. In the summertime, Jung saw his patients on the lawn of his Küsnacht house. So we were having our interview out on the lawn right beside the lake, and it was the last hour. Of course, I was feeling awful. I can't say that the transference had all been resolved or differentiated from the reality-based affection and admiration that I had for him. He had unquestionably been the most important male of that generation in my life; there is just no doubt about it. Lincoln Steffens had been up to that time the most important, but Jung superseded him and became *the* most important person that I have ever known. So I felt pretty awful, and I thought, "Well, now, I bet he is going to say something nice to me. This is the last hour, and I think he is going to lean over to me and say, 'You know, Wheelwright, I think you are going to be a wonderful analyst. I can just see it! It is written all over you!'"

But the hour went on and on, and he didn't say any such thing. It was pretty nearly time to go, and still he didn't say anything. I spread the hour out, and it went to sixty minutes; it went to sixty-five, and I thought, "Gee, if I stay any longer than this he probably won't like me, and he will be terribly angry, and he will never say anything nice to me, so I will just get up and take a chance." So I got up, and he just stuck his hand out, and said, "Goodbye, Wheelwright." That was all. I was just absolutely dashed. I shook hands with him, and I started to walk across the lawn. Then I remembered that once in Australia I had seen a slow-motion strike, so I thought, "If a striker can do it, I can do it." I began to walk in slow motion. I should have got off the lawn in about a minute at a normal walk. After what seemed half an hour—I suppose it was really about three minutes—I was running out of lawn. I was almost at the driveway when suddenly he said, "Wheelwright, come on back." I thought, "Now, now he is going to do it." I came galloping back, wagging my tail, thinking this was great, that he was going to pat me on the head and tell me what a wonderful fellow I was and what a fine analyst I would make. What he said was, "Wheelwright, when you get back to America, if you love everybody, and everybody loves you, and you are just going great guns, you had better look out. You will be in very, very bad shape indeed. Goodbye, Wheelwright." I don't know how I got across the lawn that time.

# *Postlude*

The range of foci and goals possible for Jungian analysts never ceases to amaze me. I think it fair to say that the heart of the process for most of us is the emergence of potential growth in consciousness. We are primarily oriented to health and growth, not to psychopathology. This is reflected in our terminology. Jung often said that one of his biggest debts to Freud was that he explored psychopathology so exhaustively that it left him, Jung, free to explore health and its limitless possibilities.

For most of us, our only goal is for the patient to be what is in him to be. We try not to have bright ideas about our patients. When I start work with a person, I am always reminded of a statement of Michaelangelo. He said that David was in that shaft of marble and that he must be very careful in liberating him, so that he—David—could emerge unscathed. Jung said the same of *his* sculpture.

We are blessed in having no system, no set way to go about analysis, no beginning, middle, or end. This permits us to find our own way and to function according to our temperaments. The interesting thing is that we all get reasonably good results as long as we remember that there is no *right* way to do analysis but only a right way for each one of us.

# Index

adaptation, 10, 17-19, 60, 63
Adler, Alfred, 4, 97-98
adolescence, 46, 96
*Affairs of Susan, The* (American film), 39
affect, 16
aging, 82-96
Aitutaki, 60-61
Alexander, Franz, 86
*Alice in Wonderland* (Carroll), 66
Amazon, 38, 59
America. *See* United States
analysis, 8, 10-11, 26-35, 25. *See also* relationship, therapeutic; training, analytic
analysis, Freudian, 9, 31, 33, 66-67; and psychopathology, 55, 103; and women, 79-80

analysis, Jungian, 15, 16, 31-33, 55, 80; case studies in, 17-21, 43-52, 85-87, 93-95; goals of, 18-19, 20, 22, 94-95, 103-4
analyst, 7, 8, 29-35, 56, 86
Andromeda, 39
anima/animus, 37-38, 42, 79; development of, 43-52, 87; functions of, 23-25; images of, 38-41; and psychological types, 48, 75, 80; in relationship, 20, 23-24, 44, 48-52, 83, 86-87
anonymity, 31
archetypes, 19, 25, 30, 41; and collective unconscious, 15, 16, 33, 38
assimilation, 16, 22, 24, 40-41
autoerotism, 24, 40